LEADERSHIP
IN WAR

ALSO BY ANDREW ROBERTS

The Holy Fox: A Biography of Lord Halifax

Eminent Churchillians

Salisbury: Victorian Titan

Napoleon and Wellington: The Long Duel

Hitler and Churchill: Secrets of Leadership

A History of the English-Speaking Peoples Since 1900

*Masters and Commanders: How Four Titans
Won the War in the West, 1941–1945*

The Storm of War: A New History of the Second World War

Waterloo: Napoleon's Last Gamble

Napoleon the Great

Elegy: The First Day on the Somme

Churchill: Walking with Destiny

LEADERSHIP
IN WAR

LESSONS FROM THOSE
WHO MADE HISTORY

ANDREW ROBERTS

ALLEN LANE
an imprint of
PENGUIN BOOKS

ALLEN LANE

UK | USA | Canada | Ireland | Australia
India | New Zealand | South Africa

Allen Lane is part of the Penguin Random House group of companies
whose addresses can be found at global.penguinrandomhouse.com

First published in the United States of America by Viking,
an imprint of Penguin Random House, 2019
This edition published 2019
001

Set in 11.29/18.12 pt Janson Text LT Std by Jouve (UK), Milton Keynes
Printed and bound in Great Britain by Clays Ltd, Elcograf S.p.A.

A CIP catalogue record for this book is available from the British Library

ISBN: 978–0–241–33599–4

www.greenpenguin.co.uk

MIX
Paper from
responsible sources
FSC® C018179

Penguin Random House is committed to a
sustainable future for our business, our readers
and our planet. This book is made from Forest
Stewardship Council® certified paper.

To Lew and Louise Lehrman,

my great benefactors and friends

CONTENTS

THE LEADERSHIP
CONUNDRUM

How can one hundred people be led by a single person?" That was one of the essay questions in my three-hour Cambridge University entrance exam in 1981. It is a question that has fascinated me ever since. Ultimately, it is the art of leadership that explains how not merely one hundred people, but sometimes a hundred thousand, or a million—or in China's or India's case a billion—men and women can ultimately be led, for good or ill.

This book started as a series of lectures I gave about how war demands and reveals the best and worst in leadership. I decided to focus on nine great—as in the sense of important—leaders and draw out those aspects of their personalities that reveal their leadership in the belief that there is enough in common to understand essential leadership lessons that would be applicable in more peaceful times.

We tend to think of leadership as inherently a good thing, but as the essays on Adolf Hitler and Joseph Stalin point out, it is in fact completely morally neutral, as capable of leading mankind to the abyss as to the sunlit uplands. It is a protean force of terrifying power, and perhaps one day we will rue the fact that there was ever a way that even one hundred people could be led anywhere by a single person. In the meantime, as with lethal diseases or nuclear fission, we clearly need to understand its power and try to direct it toward good, as the other seven subjects of these essays did.

Each of these nine leaders had a profound sense of self-belief, an attribute that is central to great war leadership. In some cases, as in Winston Churchill's, it stemmed from a family lineage and education that had emphasized his specialness from birth and his right to lead and rule. In others, such as Napoleon's, it stemmed from a growing realization in adolescence and early adulthood of his own remarkable intellect and capabilities. Margaret Thatcher knew by early middle age that she could lead in a way that the men around her seemed incapable of doing. Hitler's sense of self-belief grew from a recognition of the effect his words of hatred and resentment could have in rabble-rousing crowds of unemployed ex-soldiers in Bavarian beer halls in the early 1920s. Nor were setbacks allowed to dash the hopes of these leaders; rather, they tended to be used to steel them. Failure was an incident, often one that provided a lesson for the future; it was not terminal.

All of these leaders also believed they had a task to achieve, and often it was more than simply winning the war they were fighting: For Stalin it was to spread Marxism-Leninism across the globe; for Nelson the utter destruction of the principles of the French Revolution; for Hitler the triumph of the Aryan peoples through the subjection of all others. They all failed, as did Winston Churchill in his dream to prevent what he called the liquidation of the British empire, but Charles de Gaulle succeeded in his aim of restoring French honor after the catastrophe of 1940, Margaret Thatcher succeeded in reversing the seemingly irreversible decline of Britain, and Dwight Eisenhower succeeded in liberating Western Europe.

The book follows roughly chronologically because some of these leaders learned from earlier ones: The thread through Nelson to Churchill to Thatcher, for example, is a clear one, as is the one from Napoleon to Churchill. Almost all of these leaders—Stalin being the only exception—read deeply in history and biography when they were young, and were able to place themselves in the continuums of the heroes of their countries. Even Adolf Hitler saw himself as a second Arminius, and code-named his invasion of Russia after the twelfth-century German emperor Frederick I, known as Barbarossa.

When awarding Medals of Honor, President Richard Nixon noted in his book *Leaders* "how many of those who won it must have appeared to be quite ordinary people until they had risen with supreme valor to an extraordinary challenge. Without the challenge they would not have shown their courage." He concluded that "in leaders the challenge of war brings forth qualities we can readily measure. The challenges of peace may be as great, but the leader's triumph over them is neither as dramatic nor as clearly visible." It would be next to impossible, therefore, for a prime minister of Luxembourg in a time of peace to be a truly great historical leader. That might be a doleful comment on the human condition, but it is so.

LEADERSHIP
IN WAR

CHAPTER ONE

NAPOLEON BONAPARTE

1769–1821

On Thursday, June 13, 1793, a slim twenty-three-year-old artillery lieutenant stepped ashore at the port of Toulon in the south of France having escaped from a political maelstrom on his homeland island of Corsica. Napoleon Bonaparte was a penniless, almost friendless, refugee, with a mother and six siblings to support. Yet six years later he became First Consul and dictator of France, and five years after that emperor of the French. Soon afterward he made France indisputably the most powerful nation on the Continent. How did he do it?

Part of the explanation was undoubtedly luck: Napoleon was fortunate to be nineteen years old when the French Revolution broke out, allowing him to rise up the ranks of the French Army to become a general at the age of only twenty-four, in part because the aristocrats who had hitherto officered the French Army had either fled the country or been guillotined. Napoleon's own noble background in Corsica was enough to allow him to be educated for free in pre-Revolutionary France, but not enough to send him to the tumbrels.

As well as luck, there was Napoleon's own fine sense of political and military timing and his utter ruthlessness—he was ready to kill three hundred Frenchmen who were attempting an insurrection in the streets of Paris in 1795. Yet ultimately his success depended on his techniques of leadership, which allowed him to become, in Winston Churchill's words, "the greatest man of action born in Europe since Julius Caesar."[1]

That reference to Caesar was apposite because Napoleon's leadership techniques were carefully copied from his heroes of the Ancient World. Napoleon was an omnivorous reader from childhood and devoured historical and military biographies in his father's large library in Corsica and then at the three French military academies at which he studied from the age of nine. He came to see himself as a direct descendant, at least in terms of European imperial leadership, of Julius Caesar and Alexander the Great. This would imply a prima facie case of psychological disorder in most people, except that today Napoleon is indeed seen as one of the seven classical great captains of history, alongside Alexander, Caesar, Hannibal, Gustavus Adolphus, Frederick the Great, and the 1st Duke of Marlborough.

Napoleon had an extraordinary ability to inspire the soldiers of what he dubbed his Grande Armée to the extent that they would literally follow him anywhere. This would eventually include across the sands of Egyptian deserts, into almost every capital city of Europe, and through Russia's frozen wastelands. "No-one who has not experienced it can have any idea of the enthusiasm that burst forth among the half-starved, exhausted soldiers when the Emperor was there in person," a French sergeant recalled of the Battle of Leipzig in 1813. "If all were demoralised and he appeared, his presence was like an electric shock. All shouted 'Vive l'Empereur!' and everyone charged blindly into the fire."[2] Small wonder, therefore, that Wellington considered that Napoleon's mere presence on a battlefield was worth the equivalent of twenty thousand men.

Napoleon recognized that the best way to inspire his people was through two means: imbuing people with the belief that they were fighting for honor and ideology, and rewarding good work. "In my opinion the French do not care for liberty and equality, they have but one sentiment, that of honour," he said. More practically, he added that "the soldier demands glory, distinction, rewards."[3] He thus gave rewards liberally to his bravest troops in the shape of medals, pensions, promotions, lands, and titles.

Meritocracy was one of the greatest inventions of the French Revolution, unleashing the talent of a generation that had hitherto been held back by the rigid class system of the ancien régime. For centuries before 1789, Frenchmen were unlikely to rise in life much further than their fathers and grandfathers, yet suddenly meritocracy permitted talented people to reach the very apex of society. Of the twenty-six marshals of the First Empire appointed by Napoleon, ten had risen from the ranks, and they included the son of a cooper (Michel Ney), a tanner (Laurent Saint-Cyr), a bailiff (Claude Victor Perrin), a brewer (Nicolas Oudinot), a peasant (Édouard Mortier), a miller (François Lefebvre), an innkeeper (Joachim Murat), a household servant (Pierre Augereau), and a storekeeper-smuggler (André Masséna). Indeed, one might even bring the number up to eleven because although Jean Sérurier proudly boasted to have a father who was in royal service, he had in fact been the royal mole-catcher. Because of their brilliance on the battlefield, all but one of the marshals became dukes, several of them also became princes, and Murat became king of Naples and Jean-Baptiste Bernadotte king of Sweden. The saying was attributed to Napoleon that every soldier carried in his knapsack the baton of a marshal of France. Such a thing was unimaginable before the Revolution, and it partly explains the determination of the other European powers to try to crush Revolutionary and subsequently Napoleonic France.

Napoleon believed in rewarding service. He invented the Légion d'Honneur to reward both soldiers and civilians of his First Empire, which underlined his belief that honor was the primary sentiment that motivated at least the former. After the successful storming of the town of Landshut in Bavaria in 1809, for example, he asked the colonel of the 13th Infanterie Légère (Light Infantry) who had been the bravest man in the unit. The colonel hesitated, thinking it invidious to pick any particular man in an officers' mess full of heroes, so Napoleon asked the officers, who fell similarly silent. Finally an elderly captain replied that it had been the drum major who had shown the greatest courage in the storming of the city. "You have been designated the bravest in a brave regiment," Napoleon told the drum major, to cheers from the men, and he made him a chevalier in the Légion d'Honneur on the spot.[4] After the Battle of Ratisbon, a veteran asked Napoleon for the cross of the Légion d'Honneur, claiming that he had given him a watermelon at Jaffa on the Syrian campaign when it "was so terribly hot." Napoleon refused him on such a paltry pretext, at which the veteran added indignantly, "Well, don't you reckon seven wounds received at the bridge of Arcole, at Lodi and Castiglione, at the Pyramids, at Acre, Austerlitz, Friedland; eleven campaigns in Italy, Egypt, Austria, Prussia, Poland . . . !" at which a laughing emperor cut him short and also made him a chevalier of the légion with a 1,200-franc pension, fastening the cross onto his breast there and then.

If Napoleon witnessed a particular act of bravery, he would on occasion take his own medal of the légion off his uniform and present it to the soldier concerned. One can imagine the pride that such a gesture would engender in that soldier, probably for life, and the even more useful envy it would arouse among the man's comrades, eager for a similarly signal sign of the emperor's approbation. "It was by familiarities of this kind that the Emperor made the soldiers adore him," noted General Marbot, "but it was a means available only to a commander whom frequent victories had made illustrious: any other general would have injured his reputation by it."[5]

Unlike some commanders, such as the duke of Wellington, who regarded most of his men as what he called the "scum of the earth" (while not denigrating their fighting abilities), Napoleon genuinely liked spending time with his men. He had an almost democratic openness that endeared him to them. So long as they were not overtly rude, they were permitted to call out to him directly from the ranks, to question him, and to ask him for favors.

Of course not all such requests could be fulfilled, and it would have lessened their impact if they had been. Not all could have prizes. Napoleon's court chamberlain, Louis-François de Bausset, recalled how the emperor "heard, interrogated, and decided at once; if it was a refusal, the reasons were explained in a manner which softened the disappointment."[6] During one campaign a soldier came up to him asking for a new uniform, pointing to his ragged coat. "Oh no," replied Napoleon, "that would never do. It will hinder your wounds from being seen."[7] Such immediate accessibility to the commander in chief is impossible to conceive in the Legitimist armies of Prussia, Austria, or Russia, but in post-Revolutionary France it was a useful way of keeping Napoleon in touch with the needs and concerns of his men.

Napoleon always read petitions from soldiers and civilians, and granted as many as he reasonably could within France's budget. As First Consul at inspection parades at the Tuileries—which could last up to five hours—he would inquire in great detail about the men's food, uniforms, health, living quarters, amusements, cooking pots, brandy flasks, and regularity of pay, and he expected to be told the truth. (He was particularly obsessed with the state of his men's shoes and boots throughout his career; his was of course an army that did a good deal of marching across Europe.) "Conceal from me none of your wants," he told the 17th Demi-Brigade, "suppress no complaints you have to make of your superiors. I am here to do justice to all, and the weaker party is especially entitled to my protection."[8] The assumption that *le petit caporal* was on their side against *les gros bonnets* (big hats) was held throughout the army. "Pay great attention to the soldiers, and see about them in detail," Napoleon ordered Marshal Marmont in 1803 when Marmont's corps was based at Utrecht.

> The first time you arrive at the camp, line up the battalions, and spend eight hours at a stretch seeing the soldiers one by one; receive their complaints, inspect their weapons, and make sure they lack nothing. There are many advantages to making these reviews of seven to eight hours; the soldier becomes accustomed to being armed and on duty, it proves to him that the leader is paying attention to and taking complete care of him; which is a great confidence-inspiring motivation for the soldier.[9]

Napoleon cemented his popularity in the eyes of his men by doing his best to take care of them when they were wounded or ill. The horrors of late-eighteenth-century military hospitals were never far from his troops' thoughts, and Napoleon paid attention to his doctors' requirements, at least by the generally low standards of the day. In 1812 Count Philippe de Ségur, his aide-de-camp, noted how "if he happened to meet with convoys of wounded he stopped them, informed himself of their condition, of their sufferings, of the actions in which they had been wounded, and never quitted them without consoling them by his words or making them partakers in his bounty."[10]

"The tone which the officers, and sometimes even the soldiers, assumed towards the head of the government would have been indecent in any other nation," recalled the Saxon cavalry commander Baron von Odeleben, "but it was not so with the French, whose character is naturally vehement. An officer, whom Napoleon had perhaps reproached with the failure of some enterprise, might be seen defending himself from his horse on the parade, in the presence of a hundred persons composed of generals and other officers, with a vivacity and gestures which occasioned some alarm on his account. But Napoleon took no notice of these acts of presumption, and remained silent."[11] On one occasion in the extremely harsh 1813 campaign in Germany, when Napoleon had complained to General Horace Sebastiani that he commanded a "mob, not soldiers," Sebastiani flatly contradicted him, and was supported by General Jacques Macdonald, "and both together succeeded in reducing the Emperor to silence, while [the Marquis de] Caulaincourt, to avoid the disgrace of the occurrence, begged all those who were present to depart."[12] Napoleon had recognized that he had gone too far and forbore to act like a dictator in front of his senior commanders. If any anecdote was needed to explode the ludicrous view that Napoleon and Hitler were similar, that is it. Such a response from underlings toward the Führer would not have been countenanced for a moment, and retribution would have been swift and profoundly unpleasant.

Napoleon tweaked his soldiers' earlobes (sometimes quite painfully), joked, and reminisced with them and was constantly inquiring about their conditions of service. His guiding principle was "Severe to the officers, kindly to the men."[13] This stemmed partly from the knowledge that he knew that the troops appreciated the way he seemed to prefer them to his officers, but also from the knowledge that since the Revolution, the army was the citizenry in arms—raised by the *levée en masse* (mass uprising)—and so ordinary soldiers had much more political influence than before 1789. They were going to be the people on whom his political power ultimately depended. Napoleon thus meant what he said and worked hard to ensure that his men's needs were met. When campaign marches halted for lunch, he and his chief of staff, Marshal Alexandre Berthier, would invite the aides-de-camp and orderlies to eat with them. Bausset recalled this practice as "truly a fête for every one of us."[14] Napoleon also always made sure that wine from his own table was given to the sentries outside his door. These were small things, perhaps, which cost Napoleon little, but they were deeply appreciated and inspired lifelong devotion among the old *grognards* (translatable as "grumblers," but also "veterans").

Napoleon had a capacious memory for faces and names. It was highly flattering to his troops that their emperor recognized them and singled them out, reminiscing about past battles and constantly asking them questions. Nor did such familiarity ever breed contempt in them, but merely loyalty. Of course efficient staff work helped in Napoleon's ability to "recognize" individual *grognards* in the ranks, but he also deployed his phenomenal memory. "I introduced three parliamentary deputies of the Valais region to him," Jean-Antoine Chaptal, Napoleon's interior minister, recalled in his memoirs:

> he asked one of them about his two little girls. This deputy told me that he had only seen Napoleon once, at the foot of the Alps, when he went to [fight the Battle of] Marengo. Problems with the artillery, added the deputy, forced him to stop for a moment in front of his house; he petted his two children, mounted his horse, and since then he had not seen him again.[15]

That incident had taken place a full ten years before.

Napoleon's memory was put to full use when it came to military dispositions. In 1812 he dictated the complete war establishment for the army to General Mathieu Dumas, the intendant general of the army (and grandfather of the novelist Alexandre

———

Dumas). This incorporated where all the conscripts needed to go and the effective force of all the corps of the army. "He walked rapidly up and down, or stood still before the window of his cabinet" for half an hour, Dumas recalled, and "dictated with such rapidity that I had scarcely time to set down the figures clearly." Dumas finally looked up and realized that the emperor had achieved this formidable task entirely without reference to the table of notes he had been given. "You thought that I was reading your table," Napoleon said. "I don't want it; I know it by heart. Let us go on."[16]

Dumas was also astonished by the way that Napoleon could demonstrate intuitive foresight about how campaigns would develop, a hugely important quality in any war leader. In October 1800 he spoke to Dumas of his plans for attacking the Austrians in the Tyrol, telling him, as they looked together at a giant map of the Alps from the Rhine to the River Adige:

> We shall deprive them, and almost without fighting, of this immense fortress of the Tyrol; we must manoeuvre on their flanks, and threaten their last point of retreat; they will then immediately evacuate all the upper valleys. . . . I well see that there are difficulties, in all probability greater than at any other point in the chain of the Great Alps. But I hold that there are no asperities on the globe which man cannot surmount. Tell [General] Macdonald that an army can pass always, and at all seasons, wherever two men can set their feet. . . . It is

not by the numerical force of an army, but by the object, the importance of the operation, that I measure that of the command.[17]

Napoleon's regular proclamations and Orders of the Day greatly inspired his troops. They were phrased in a classical style that sounds florid to modern ears, even belabored, but which sounded majestic at the time, especially when read around the campfire by noncommissioned officers to their largely illiterate rank and file. "Remember from those monuments yonder," Napoleon famously proclaimed on the morning of the Battle of the Pyramids in 1798, "forty centuries look down upon you."[18] The day after the Battle of Abensberg at the start of the 1809 campaign against the Hapsburg empire, he told his troops, "The fire of Heaven, which punished the ungrateful, the unjust, the disloyal, has struck the Austrian army."[19]

Proclamations and bulletins were very often not true in the literal sense, in that Napoleon used them for propaganda, and certainly no numbers in them could be trusted. "To lie like a bulletin" even entered the French idiom, but such exaggerations were taken for granted, rather as Jacques-Louis David's painting of Napoleon crossing the Alps on a rearing horse was not intended to be thought historically accurate, either. Artistic license was as evident in inspiring proclamations as in art itself.

Napoleon inspired his men verbally, too, as when he delivered a speech to the grenadiers, encouraging them to brave Austrian fire as they were about to storm the long narrow bridge across the River Adda during the Battle of Lodi in the first campaign in which he was commander in chief. "One must speak to the soul," he later said of that occasion; "it is the only way to electrify the men."[20] When in the Eylau-Friedland campaign of 1807 Napoleon told the 44th Line Regiment, "Your three battalions could be as six in my eyes," they shouted back: "And we shall prove it!"[21] This was the classic expression of the concept of esprit de corps, also known at the time as the Sacred Fire, the French fury (by their enemies), and summed up in the word *élan*.

A good way of speaking to the soul and electrifying the men was to add words of glory to their regimental battle honors after engagements in which they had distinguished themselves. In the Italian campaign, for example, Napoleon gave certain demi-brigades the opportunity to distinguish themselves on parade. In March 1797 he approved the 57th Demi-Brigade's right to stitch in gold onto their colors the words THE TERRIBLE 57TH DEMI-BRIGADE WHICH NOTHING CAN STOP, because of their courage at the battles of Rivoli and La Favorita in Italy. Such names stitched onto the standards of certain demi-brigades—such as LES INCOMPARABLES (9th Légère)—showed how fundamentally Napoleon understood the psychology of the ordinary soldier and the power of regimental pride.[22] The 18th Line Regiment was called Les Braves for their battlefield performance at the Battle of Aspern-Essling, which they thereafter repeated often, especially at Borodino. The 84th Line was given the soubriquet "Un Contre Dix" ("One Against Ten") in 1809 for defeating a force of Tyrolean rebels estimated at ten times their number. Any soldiers in any army throughout history have been enthused by the slightest distinction that lifts them above the rest.

Yet Napoleon could be harsh with his men, too. Leaders need to understand mass psychology and he recognized that shame could occasionally work almost as well as lavishing praise and heaping rewards on troops. "Soldiers of the 39th and 85th Infantry Regiments," he once told two units of the French Army serving in Italy—known as the Army of Italy—that had fled during a battle in 1796:

> you are no longer fit to belong to the French Army. You have shown neither discipline nor courage; you have allowed the enemy to dislodge you from a position where a handful of brave men could have stopped an army. The Chief of Staff will cause to be inscribed upon your flags: "These men are no longer of The Army of Italy."[23]

With his acute sense for what would energize and what demoralize a unit, Napoleon correctly gauged that this public humiliation would ensure that both demi-brigades would fight harder and with more determination over the coming battles in order to regain their good name. He knew that this would not have worked unless they had a sense of collective self-identity, which was always the primary purpose of the demi-brigade, just as it was of the regiment in the British Army.

Napoleon had learned that leadership lesson from Julius Caesar. He recounted in his book *Caesar's Wars* the story of a mutiny in Rome in which Caesar had agreed laconically to his soldiers' demands for release from service, but afterward addressed them with ill-concealed contempt merely as "citizens" rather than as the customary "soldiers" or "comrades," and how, "finally, the result of this moving scene was to win the continuation of their services."[24]

Napoleon ensured that plays were written to glorify the Grande Armée, songs and operatic arias sung, proclamations made, festivals inaugurated, ceremonies held, standards and medals distributed. He designed glorious uniforms for his army, to encourage esprit, differentiate units from afar, and impress the opposite sex. ("Rarely has a more colourful band of warriors been assembled in a single generation, army or country," wrote the historian Dr. David Chandler.)[25]

Napoleon instinctively understood the power of symbols and what soldiers wanted.[26] Above all, at least until the Battle of Aspern-Essling in 1809, he gave them what they wanted more than anything else: victory. Yet even when things had clearly gone badly wrong Napoleon's army stayed loyal to him far longer than any other body in the rest of French society.

The Swiss military historian General Antoine-Henri de Jomini, who served in both the French and Russian armies during the Napoleonic Wars, was greatly impressed by the way that Napoleon understood "that it is necessary never to inspire too much contempt for the enemy, because should you find an obstinate resistance, the morale of the soldier might be shaken by it."[27] Instead, Napoleon openly recognized the worth of enemy units, thereby increasing his troops' morale when they overcame them. In the 1806 campaign against Prussia, Napoleon praised the enemy cavalry to one French corps, although he took care to promise "it could do nothing against the bayonets of his Egyptians!"*[28]

Napoleon would also praise enemy generals he despised and ignore ones he admired in the hope that the bad ones would be promoted and the good ones dismissed. In the Italian campaign of 1796–97, Napoleon recognized that Field Marshal József Alvinczi was the best general Austria had, which was why he never mentioned him in his bulletins, while he praised Generals Johann Beaulieu and Dagobert von Wurmser and Archduke Charles Hapsburg, whom he knew he could beat. He also showed great respect to General Giovanni di Provera in his proclamations and Orders of the Day, whom he privately thought the worst of all.

Praise of his own soldiers was by no means directed solely to the rank and file. "My trust in you is as great as my appreciation of your military talents," he once wrote to Marshal Bessières, "your courage and your love of order and discipline."[29] Overall, however, he was much harder on the marshalate and the upper ranks than on the ordinary soldier, and toward the end of his career he worried—with reason—that his scorn had curtailed

---

* Napoleon was referring to his veterans who had fought in Egypt.

the marshals' capacity for independent action. "I have accustomed them too much to knowing only how to obey," he complained in 1813.[30]

MUCH OF NAPOLEON'S extraordinary capacity for work derived from his ability to compartmentalize his mind, to concentrate entirely on whatever problem was before him, to the exclusion of all else. "Different subjects and different affairs are arranged in my head as in a cupboard," he once said. "When I wish to interrupt one train of thought, I shut that drawer and open another. Do I wish to sleep? I simply close all the drawers, and there I am—asleep."[31]

He nonetheless had relatively little time to sleep, regularly working up to eighteen hours a day. He used every moment he could find, spending a maximum of only half an hour over meals and having newspapers read to him while he was in the bath and shaving. Some of his twenty-two mistresses complained about how little time he spent in foreplay, and when he met civil servants he was uncommonly direct with them. "Where are we with the Arc de Triomphe?" he would demand of his architect, and "Will I walk on the Jena bridge on my return?"[32]

One aspect of Napoleon's leadership that proved essential, especially in the retreats and defeats of the latter part of his reign, was his Olympian calmness under pressure. "In my own case it's taken me years to cultivate self-control to prevent my emotions from betraying themselves," he said in 1813.

Only a short time ago I was the conqueror of the world, commanding the largest and finest army of modern times. That's all gone now! To think I kept all my composure, I might even say preserved my unvarying high spirits. . . . Yet don't think that my heart is less sensitive than those of other men. I'm a very kind man but since my earliest youth I have devoted myself to silencing that chord within me that never yields a sound now. If anyone told me when I was about to begin a battle that my mistress whom I loved to distraction was breathing her last, it would leave me cold. Yet my grief would be just as great as if I'd given way to it . . . and after the battle I should mourn my mistress if I had the time. Without all this self-control, do you think I could have done all I've done?[33]

This self-control allowed Napoleon to crack jokes during the battles of Marengo in Italy in 1800 and Wagram in Austria in 1809, even when shot and shell were flying around him.

To achieve success on the battlefield, it was not necessary for Napoleon to invent new strategies and tactics for the French Army: Instead he brilliantly adapted the new thinking of others for the wars he had to fight. Tactical formations such as the *battalion carré* (square battalion) and the *ordre mixte* (mixed order) were the concepts of French military thinkers dating from the aftermath of France's defeat in the Seven Years' War, as was the corps system that Napoleon perfected to move bodies of men of

twenty thousand to forty thousand with exceptional effective-
ness during a campaign. From 1812 (when Napoleon's enemies
also adopted it) until 1945 the corps system remained central to
European war making. Leaders do not necessarily have to have
good ideas themselves, but they do need to be able to spot the
good from the bad, and adopt and adapt the former.

One of Napoleon's hallmarks—at least in his early
campaigns—was speed, just as it had been with Julius Caesar
and was to be with the Wehrmacht in 1940–41. *"Activité, activité, vitesse!* [Action, action, speed!]" Napoleon ordered André
Masséna.[34] Wherever possible he attempted to avoid long sieges
(one of the characteristics of seventeenth- and eighteenth-century
warfare), to live off the land, and, crucially, to retain the initiative. In 1805 the use of corps allowed him to move the Grande
Armée from their cantonments on the Channel coast to Ulm
on the River Danube in a matter of weeks, completely outma-
neuvering his Austrian enemy. By 1812, however, the Grande
Armée had grown too big for that kind of lightning campaigning to be possible. The army with which Napoleon invaded
Russia numbered 615,000—roughly the same size as the population of Paris. Generals entered Russia in their domestic car-
riages, taking their evening dress, chefs, porcelain services, and
so on. The days of dash and tactical flexibility in attack seen in
the Italian campaign of 1796–97 were over, and in that sense
Napoleon's ultimate downfall was a result of too much success
earlier on.

What was also seen in Italy was Napoleon's vicious destruction of resistance to his rule, especially at Pavia in 1796. Great leaders occasionally need to be utterly ruthless, as Oliver Cromwell was at Drogheda and Wexford in 1649, Admiral Nelson was in Naples in 1799, and Winston Churchill and President Roosevelt were over the Combined Bomber Offensive in the Second World War. For Napoleon the "whiff of grapeshot" in Paris in 1795, the bloody pacification of Pavia, and above all the punishment of Jaffa in 1799—where he had around three thousand Turkish prisoners of war massacred by bullet and bayonet on the beach outside the city—were the moments that he descended to the use of sheer terror to win his campaign and terrify local populations into no longer opposing him. For all that he was thoughtful and considerate while looking after his own army, he could on short and isolated occasions resort to terror tactics. These almost always rebounded badly against the French Army, especially in Spain during the Peninsular campaign, when they prompted torture on a large scale against captured French soldiers. The cruelty that Napoleon showed was, however, on an ad hoc basis, and certainly not built into the entire ethos of his government, as for example the massacring of millions was for Stalin's rule.

Napoleon's decision to invade Russia in 1812 was in retrospect of course disastrous, but it was much more rational than it seems with the benefit of hindsight of that catastrophic campaign. Napoleon had beaten the Russians twice before in the Austerlitz campaign in 1805 and the Eylau-Friedland campaign in 1807. He wanted only a short, sharp campaign on Russia's borders and never intended to penetrate deep inside Russia, let alone go all the way to Moscow. His army was over twice the size of the Russian Army at the start of the campaign; indeed, it was the largest invasion force in the history of mankind to that point, comprising an exceptionally broad coalition of no fewer than twenty-one states. The disease that destroyed much of the central column of his invasion—typhus—was not to be diagnosed until 1911. Furthermore, it was not true that he did not know about the harshness of the Russian winter. A highly intelligent and well-read man, Napoleon had studied the disastrous campaign of King Charles XII of Sweden, as recounted by Voltaire. He, therefore, allowed more time to get back from Moscow to Smolensk than it had taken to get from Smolensk to Moscow.

He could have stopped at Vitebsk or Smolensk on the way into Russia, but it seemed to make little sense to halt at Vitebsk in July when he had advanced 190 miles in a month and suffered fewer than ten thousand battle casualties. Audacity had always served him well up until then, and he would cede the initiative if he stopped at Vitebsk so early in the year. Czar Alexander I had called up the 80,000-strong militia in Moscow on July 24 and was arming 400,000 serfs, so it made sense to attack before they were trained and deployed. Murat also pointed out that Russian morale must have been devastated by the constant retreats, wondering how much more of Russia could the czar see ravaged before he sued for peace. Napoleon could not have known that Alexander had declared in St. Petersburg that he would never make peace, saying: "I would sooner let my beard grow to my waist and eat potatoes in Siberia."[35]

These were all logical attitudes, not the result of the insane hubris of which Napoleon is regularly accused.* He undoubtedly made a key mistake in choosing the wrong route for the army's retreat after the Battle of Maloyaroslavets in late October 1812, but that should not lull us into thinking the whole campaign was doomed as soon as he had crossed the Niemen that June.

NAPOLEON'S CAREER from the siege of Toulon in 1793 to the disaster at Waterloo in 1815 is replete with leadership lessons, several of which will be seen in the careers of other leaders in this book. At Toulon he learned not to be afraid to take control, even from those older, senior, and more experienced officers than himself, because he knew he had the support of the overall commander. He mastered the art of working with close colleagues in a cooperative but necessarily competitive atmosphere. At the Battle of Arcola in 1796, Napoleon learned how to control the message and how what really happened is often not as important as what people think happened. A messy skir-

---

* Indeed, although there is undoubtedly such a psychological disorder as the Napoleon complex, Napoleon himself did not have one.

mish around a bridge was turned into a heroic myth, teaching Napoleon that public relations could not be ignored.

At the Brumaire coup d'état of 1799, Napoleon surrounded himself with the best people for each situation, whom he was prepared to change as the situation changed. The creation of the new honors system based on the Légion d'Honneur in 1800 allowed everyone in France to recognize that it was Napoleon himself who controlled promotions, with all the accretion of power that went with that knowledge. The establishment of the Napoleonic Code in 1804 allowed Napoleon to take the ultimate credit for the ideas and hard work of experts working under his overall supervision. Indeed, a visitor to Napoleon's tomb today might be forgiven for thinking the entire code—which still informs the French legal system today—sprang entirely from Napoleon's brain unaided.

In the Austerlitz campaign and in his escape from Elba in 1815, Napoleon showed how timing was everything. His patient study of his opponents' psychology helped him work out precisely the best moment for him to strike. In his escape from the Russian campaign and flight to Paris in 1812, Napoleon demonstrated the importance of protecting and defending his power base. On landing back at Golfe-Juan near Antibes on the southern coast on March 1, 1815, Napoleon proved that given courage and steady nerves, leaders can make extraordinary comebacks, as was seen in the careers of Churchill, de Gaulle, Richard Nixon, and others. At Laffrey six days later—where he faced down the troops sent by Louis XVIII to arrest him—Napoleon showed himself more than capable of playing on his veterans' raw emotions, appealing to the romantic streak in the French soul. He maintained his sangfroid after the allies rejected his overtures on March 13, not letting either antagonists or supporters see his inner turmoil.

The Waterloo campaign was similarly replete with leadership lessons; although he was not hubristic when he invaded Russia, he showed bad judgment after the Battle of Ligny on June 16, 1815, when he sent Marshal Emmanuel de Grouchy off to chase the Prussians with a large force that he would desperately need on the battlefield of Waterloo two days later. During June 17, as the allied army retreated in the rain, Napoleon—who once said that he could afford to lose an army but never an hour—wasted time. Leaders need to be energetic, or at least convey a sense of energy to their followers.

At the Battle of Waterloo itself, Napoleon seemed to ignore all of the military maxims that he had spent a lifetime propagating. Instead of playing to his strengths and his opponent's weaknesses, he did the opposite. He failed to retain the initiative. He delegated overall personal control, including vital decisions over the timing and direction of attacks, to lieutenants, which he had not done earlier in his career, however much he trusted them or how well they had performed in the past. He had the wrong marshals in the wrong places, and the best of all of them—Louis-Nicolas Davout—he left far away in Paris. Waterloo was an entirely atypical Napoleonic battle, and it ended in an atypical result for him: final, catastrophic defeat. Why he

failed to stick to his tried, trusted, and hitherto largely successful rules of warfare is down to several factors. They had failed
him in the 1813 campaigns in Germany; many of his best marshals had refused to rejoin the colors when he returned from
exile on Elba; he was unsure exactly where the Prussians had
retreated to after the Battle of Ligny, and guessed wrong; the
heavy rain on June 17 slowed down his army chasing Wellington's and robbed him of the initiative; his health (a severe attack
of hemorrhoids) might also have been a factor, although equally
that could have been an excuse provided afterward by his followers to explain his defeat.

For all that, it is worth recalling the leadership qualities that
Napoleon demonstrated elsewhere in his career, not least in the
forty-six battles that he won of the sixty he fought. They will be
qualities that we will encounter to a greater or lesser degree—
generally lesser—in many of the following chapters. For
Napoleon's career demonstrated the importance of compart-
mentalization, meticulous planning, knowledge of terrain, superb timing, steady nerves, valuing the importance of discipline
and training, understanding the psychology of the ordinary
soldier to create esprit de corps, the issuing of inspirational
speeches and proclamations, controlling the news, adapting the
tactical ideas of others, asking pertinent questions of the right
people, a deep learning and appreciation of history, a formidable memory, utter ruthlessness when necessary, the deployment
of personal charisma, immense calm under unimaginable pressure (especially in moments that look like defeat), an almost

obsessive-compulsive attention to detail, rigorous control of emotions, and the ability to exploit a momentary numerical advantage at the decisive point on the battlefield—and, not least, good luck. Even though he was ultimately defeated, Napoleon is the wartime leader against whom all the others must be judged.

CHAPTER TWO

HORATIO NELSON

1758–1805

Adjectives and phrases that have been applied to Admiral Lord Nelson in recent biographies, articles, and book reviews include "gauche, vain, priggish, hypochondriacal," "petulant, undignified, self-pitying," "nervy," "emotional, disappointed, irritable, embittered," "peevish," "taciturn," and "a political simpleton and an insignificant private man." Many of those are true, but he was also unquestionably the greatest military hero whom England has ever produced, indeed the very personification of heroism itself. In his brief forty-seven years, before he was shot down at the climax of his almost impossibly adventurous life, Horatio Nelson mixed fearless gallantry, unrelenting aggression, a powerful sense of duty, faith in God, hatred of the French in general and French revolutionaries in particular, and a genius for both naval strategy and tactics with monstrous vanity, ceaseless self-promotion, and a driving ambition. Yet ambition is not a sin if allied to extraordinary ability, which in his case it undoubtedly was.

Benjamin Disraeli wrote to Queen Victoria in 1879: "It is quite true that [Field Marshal Lord] Wolseley is an egotist and a braggart. So was Nelson. . . . Men of action, when eminently successful in early life, are generally boastful and full of themselves."[1] The prime minister was right to remind the queen-empress that a great man does not also have to be a sweet and modest one. Referring to oneself in the third person is an unfailing litmus test of vanity and pomposity, indeed, often of incipient megalomania, and Horatio Nelson spectacularly failed it, writing of himself that "Nelson is as far above doing a scandalous or mean action as the heavens are above the earth."[2] He also published a brief account of his own career ending with the words "Go thou and do likewise," doubtless knowing full well that no one could.[3]

Yet for all his personal failings and his infidelity to his long-suffering wife, Fanny, Horatio Nelson saved his country from a far more serious danger of invasion than even that later posed by Adolf Hitler and secured its domination of the world's oceans for more than a century. Besides these gigantic achievements, who cares about a bit of peevishness and undignified petulance? Several of more than one hundred of Nelson's biographers should get their priorities right: His story is a sublime one of patriotism, courage, and leadership, and two centuries after his death it still has the power to thrill the hearts of freedom-loving people everywhere.

Born in Burnham Thorpe in Norfolk on September 29, 1758, the fifth surviving son of its rector, Reverend Edmund Nelson, Horatio went to sea before his thirteenth birthday aboard the 64-gun warship *Raisonnable,* under the command of his maternal uncle, Captain Maurice Suckling. Although it was not unknown for young officers to go to sea as early as Nelson, he was fortunate to have his uncle as captain, who became a father figure to him. Despite the Royal Navy's being a natural career destination for a Norfolk younger son with a captain in the family, Nelson was violently seasick, a malaise that recurred throughout his career.

The Royal Navy was a tough upbringing for a boy who had lost his mother when he was nine. Ordinary Royal Navy seamen, known as ratings, though not the officers like him, were often the sweepings of the prison hulks or the gleanings of the press gangs, who deserted the moment they could. The traditions of the navy of those days have been summed up as "rum, prayers, sodomy and the lash." Sailors received a tot of rum once a day when the sun went over the yardarm and prayers were read on Sunday mornings; the rest was up to the individual.

Captain Suckling ensured the young Horatio became proficient in navigation and sailing and soon knew the pilotage of the Rivers Medway and Thames expertly. His training in practical seamanship could hardly have been better, and he was chosen for an Arctic voyage at only age fourteen, as coxswain of the captain's gig. It was there he was popularly believed to have killed a polar bear in mortal combat, although evidence for this is sketchy. On his return, he was sent by the Admiralty to the East Indies on board the 20-gun *Seahorse*, but in the course of traveling to every station from Bengal to Bassorah (modern-day Basra in Iraq), he caught malaria and had to be invalided home. "I almost wished myself overboard," he later said of this inactive time in his life.[4]

Yet as his ship rounded the Cape of Good Hope, Nelson had a strange, still-unexplained vision of "a radiant orb" and "a sudden glow," which he took to be a direct sign from the Almighty, and as he put it, "A sudden glow of patriotism was kindled within me. . . . I *will* be a hero, and confiding in Providence, I will brave every danger."[5] Nelson's powerful lifelong sense of personal destiny seems to have stemmed from this odd teenage metaphysical experience.

By April 1777 the eighteen-year-old Nelson had passed his naval examinations and been promoted to second lieutenant aboard the 32-gun frigate *Lowestoffe*, under the command of his friend Captain William Locker. Locker's military philosophy was simple: "Lay a Frenchman close and you will beat him."[6] It was supported by the practical evidence of the better-trained and -provisioned Royal Navy's being able to fire three broadsides in the same two-minute time frame that it took the French and Spanish navies to fire two. It was a fundamental lesson of warfare in the age of fighting sail that Nelson took to heart, and later exploited to the full.

After serving in Jamaica he was promoted to post-captain and—four months short of his twenty-first birthday—transferred to the flagship of the commander in chief, Sir Peter Parker. This was fast-track promotion by the standards of the navy, though by no means unknown. He rose by dint of his intelligence, application, and superb maritime ability; nor was he hindered by Suckling's promotion to the influential financial post of comptroller of the Royal Navy. Nepotism might have been an eighteenth-century disease, and is widely denounced today, but there is no escaping the fact that it greatly helped the career of our finest naval commander.

In January 1780, by then captaining a frigate, Nelson took part in the disastrous amphibious assault against the Spanish possessions of San Juan. Yellow fever killed the vast majority of the British seamen who died in that campaign, and Nelson, suffering from ague, survived it only because he was recalled to Jamaica, and afterward was ordered to return to England, where he spent a year rebuilding his health. When he did go back to sea, sailing to Canada and America, he got "knocked up with scurvy." (He wasn't impressed when he visited New York in 1783, saying that "money is the great object here. Nothing else is attended to.")[7]

Commanding the frigate HMS *Boreas* between 1784 and 1787, on an unpopular mission to prevent Britain's West Indian colonists from trading with the newly independent United States of America, he was not the compassionate commander whom Victorian and later hagiographers have made out. In his eighteen months commanding the *Boreas*, Nelson ordered the flogging of 54 of his 122 seamen and 12 of his 20 marines, an astonishing 47 percent of the entire crew. He thought Christmas Day as good as any other to hang a mutineer.

It was also as captain of the *Boreas* that Nelson met and soon afterward married a young widow from the Caribbean island of Nevis, Frances (Fanny) Nisbet, niece of the president of the Council of Nevis, in 1787. She was not a great beauty, and often shy, but a kind and loving wife who certainly did not deserve the very public humiliations that lay in store. There is no reason to suppose that Nelson did not love her when they got married, although it was a financially advantageous match for him.

There then followed six years of peace in which Nelson had to eke out an existence on half pay, living with his father and wife in Norfolk and developing the reactionary Tory views that were profoundly opposed to the precepts of the French Revolution. These went so far as to include a wholly atavistic belief in the divine right of kings. He was delighted, therefore, when in February 1793 Revolutionary France declared war on Britain only a matter of days after the execution of Louis XVI.

On the outbreak of war, Nelson was given his first large ship to command, the 64-gun frigate HMS *Agamemnon*, and ordered to join the Mediterranean fleet at Naples. On July 12, 1794, during the siege of the Corsican town of Calvi, a cannonball struck a piece of stone on the ground near where Nelson was standing, fragments from which blinded him in his right eye. (Contrary to popular belief he never wore an eye patch, but only a green shade attached to his hat.) It was in this campaign that his reputation for utter fearlessness was born. As a child he is reputed to have said to his grandmother: "Fear? I never saw fear."

Nelson emerged from this period of the war convinced that he was one of God's instruments for punishing French regicide, atheism, and egalitarianism, and he would do it through an unvarying policy of attack, characterized by repeated exhibitions of near-suicidal bravery.

The next year, after a daring and successful attack against the French outside Toulon, Admiral Sir John Jervis appointed Nelson to the rank of commodore, but it was three years later, fighting under Jervis in the Battle of Cape St. Vincent, that he displayed his flair for independent decision making. Risking court-martial and disgrace for leaving the line of battle without permission, Nelson—having spotted that the two divided sections of the Spanish fleet were about to reunite—sailed his ship, HMS *Captain*, straight into the 80-gun *San Nicolas* and led a boarding party, which captured her, becoming the first Englishman successfully to board an enemy ship of the line since Sir Edward Howard in 1513. Yet no sooner had the Spanish vessel struck her colors than Nelson proceeded to board a much larger enemy ship that had drifted alongside, the 112-gun *San Josef*, which he also captured. Jervis embraced Nelson when he went aboard the flagship after the battle; the commodore was knighted and promoted to rear admiral.

Demonstrating a flair for self-promotion that soon made him unpopular with fellow officers, Nelson sent accounts of his own valor and success back to London for maximum distribution, including in the newspapers. He didn't need to exaggerate his successes, however, and his brother officers understandably felt he left them in his shade. Nonetheless, in a Britain starved of good news, it helped turn him into a popular hero, what today would be called a celebrity.

Later, in 1797, leading an expedition to try to capture a Spanish treasure ship sheltering at Tenerife, Nelson lost his right arm to grapeshot from the fortress of Santa Cruz. It was cut off below the shoulder in an operation undertaken without anesthetic. "A left-handed admiral will never again be considered," he lamented. "I am become a burden to my friends, and useless to my country."[8] In fact, the opposite was true; to have lost both an eye and an arm in action only underlined for his men the fact that Nelson would never ask them to do something that he was not willing to undertake himself, and the nation took note.

Fanny had not seen her husband for nearly five years when he returned as Admiral Sir Horatio Nelson, hero of the Battle of Cape St. Vincent, blind in one eye and with only one arm. Fanny nursed the infected stump of his arm and due to what one biographer has called her angelic tenderness, he recovered well enough to sail off again to the Mediterranean to hunt down Napoleon's expedition to Egypt, which had left Toulon in May 1798.[9]

In England, Nelson had been on half pay, suffering from an abdominal hernia from the battle, occasionally feeling feverish, and taking laudanum (essentially opium) to dull the pain of the daily dressings that his wound required. Nelson had a slight frame, as his admiral's uniform in the National Maritime Museum at Greenwich shows. He was five feet five inches tall, had a delicate constitution, and thought of himself as never far away from death, which doubtless went toward explaining his great courage in battle.

Returning to sea again as soon as he had recovered, Nelson made an inspired guess: that Napoleon's fleet—which had slipped past the British blockade of Toulon—had headed for Egypt, and on the evening of August 1, 1798, he finally caught up with it lying at anchor at Aboukir Bay at the mouth of the Nile. "Before this time tomorrow," he told his officers on the eve of battle, "I shall have gained a peerage or Westminster Abbey."[10] Marine archaeology undertaken at the time of the battle's bicentenary has underlined how brilliant but risky Nelson's maneuver was. By sailing five ships through shallows around the head of the French line to attack from the landward side as well as the seaward, where the French had not armed their guns, Nelson won one of the most decisive victories in naval history. Bravery and luck played only a limited part in Nelson's victories; his superb seamanship and acute ability to exploit opportunities were a much more important part of his naval strategy, born of the Royal Navy's excellent on-the-job training. (In the Egyptian National Museum in Cairo are French muskets and coinage that have been brought up from the seabed.) Out of seventeen French capital ships, only four escaped, leaving the French Army utterly stranded in Asia. Nelson's headlong attack has been criticized, but he went ahead because the wind was fair and the French were unprepared, which they might not have been the next day.

After the Battle of the Nile, Nelson was indeed elevated to the peerage and deluged with valuable presents from the czar of Russia, the sultan of Turkey, the City of London, the East India Company, and so on. He was not yet forty years old, and the adulation contributed to the burgeoning of his colossal vanity. It was when he was recuperating in Naples from a severe wound to the forehead that he sustained at the Nile that he fell in love and began an affair with Emma Hamilton.

Nelson's decent, dowdy, long-suffering wife, Fanny, tended him and loved him, but when he encountered the electrifying charms of Emma, Lady Hamilton, poor Fanny didn't stand a chance. Emma was the wife of the British minister in Naples, Sir William Hamilton, an aesthete and sophisticate who was thirty-five years older than she, and perfectly amenable. At the Frick Gallery in New York, you can see George Romney's rosy-cheeked smiling Emma Hamilton, the saddest picture in the gallery when one thinks of the shambolic debt-ridden alcoholic that she became. Emma is blue eyed, peachy skinned, and happy, with a turquoise ribbon in her hair and a trusting smile. It is easy to see how Nelson—and everyone else—fell for her so instantaneously, although there was never any question of their being able to live together, given the social and religious mores of the day.

One problem in describing Emma Hamilton is that she changed so much during her life, altering herself with her circumstances. Against Romney's beautiful portrait of Emma at the Frick, we have the diplomat Sir Gilbert Elliot, later 1st Earl of Minto, saying that she had a figure that was "nothing short of monstrous in its enormity, and the easygoing manner of a barmaid." As for the songs that she insisted on singing at dinners in Nelson's honor, the socialite Lady Holland described them as "vile discordant screaming." Emma would perform cringe-makingly embarrassing impromptu dances, too. "It was certainly not of a nature to be performed except before a select company," recorded one guest, "as the screams, attitudes, starts and embraces with which it was interrupted gave it a peculiar character." Despite all this, she was undoubtedly extremely sexy, and ensorcelled Nelson with ease. A modern biographer of Nelson, John Sugden, describes the young Lady Hamilton as "an arresting presence in the prime of life, tall, strong-limbed, voluptuous, her stunningly beautiful countenance as expressive and commanding as it was classical, cast with an enormous angry auburn mane, and all held in the service of an energetic, vibrant, and often tempestuous personality. She was constitutionally histrionic, besotted with attention, noise and company, in which she thrived and shone."[11]

Emma encouraged Nelson's sense of self-importance. Indeed, when he complained that he had been made only a baron, the lowest rank in the order of peerage, she told him she would not be content until he was also "Marquis Nile, Viscount Pyramid and Baron Crocodile."

When Nelson finally returned to Britain from Naples, he

was an adored national figure. Ladies wore bonnets with THE HERO OF THE NILE embroidered in sequins. When he toured the countryside, workingmen would unharness his horses and pull his carriage along themselves. He loved all this and actively manipulated his image, sanctioning idealized portraits and prints that looked absolutely nothing like him. He rode in triumph in the Lord Mayor's show, yet was received coldly at court by King George III, who prized marital fidelity, and—most unusual for the Hanoverians—even practiced it personally. This did not hinder Nelson's professional advancement, however, since admirals who brought great victories were prized by everyone.

For all Nelson's genius at sea, nothing could be done by Britain to hinder Napoleon's domination of a land empire comprising much of the western half of the European continent, and Britain still stood in danger of invasion from Napoleon's huge Grande Armée soon to be stationed in the Channel ports. In order to maintain the blockade of France, it became necessary to attack the Danish fleet at Copenhagen in April 1801. Vice Admiral Lord Nelson was second in command to Admiral Parker, and when, fearing mounting costs from the shore batteries, Nelson was ordered to "discontinue the action," he simply ignored it and fought on through to total victory. (The phrase "to turn a blind eye" refers to this incident, in which Nelson is popularly believed to have put his telescope to his blind eye and joked: "I really do not see the signal." Sadly, it is untrue.)

As at Cape St. Vincent, the subsequent victory completely

vindicated this act of gross insubordination, but it did not make him popular with all his fellow admirals. Nelson's own commanding officer and mentor, the earl of St. Vincent, later wrote that "animal courage was the sole merit of Lord Nelson, his private character most disgraceful, in every sense of the word." Yet he nonetheless also said that Nelson "possessed the magic art of infusing his own spirit into others."[12] This was key to Nelson's war leadership: He was loved by ordinary seamen in the fleet and had the ability to inspire others, sometimes simply by his mere presence at an action. Not for nothing has he been described as "a natural-born predator."[13] This popularity with the seamen was all the more remarkable in a tough disciplinarian, yet he gave them victory (and thus also prize money).

Against this love of Nelson must be set the accusation that he was responsible for a heinous war crime in Naples in late June 1799. There is little doubt that Nelson's actions led directly to the executions in cold blood of ninety-nine Italian pro-Jacobin prisoners of war after the British commander on the spot, Captain Edward Foote, had signed a treaty guaranteeing their safety once they had surrendered. Certainly, when one visits the near-impregnable Castel dell'Ovo in Naples today, one immediately recognizes how hard it would have been to capture if the rebels had not voluntarily surrendered it.

Nelson's supporters maintain that it wasn't exactly a treaty, that Foote had no authority to sign it in any case, that it was the Neapolitan royalists rather than the British who had found the

Jacobins guilty after a proper court-martial, that the victims were legally rebels rather than genuine soldiers and thus later prisoners of war, and so on, but as the British Whig leader Charles James Fox pointed out, Nelson's behavior did "stain the British name." This was underlined when Nelson refused to allow a Christian burial for the rebel naval commander, Commodore Francesco Caracciolo, after he was hanged from the yardarm, ordering instead that the corpse be merely weighted down and tossed into the sea.* Emma's bloodthirstiness in toasting the man's death was equally distasteful.

Nelson's biographer Tom Pocock concludes that it was Caracciolo's "misfortune that his path crossed Nelson's at a time when the latter was displaying an uncharacteristic ruthlessness in carrying out the cruel customs of war."[14] Nelson saw himself as acting on behalf of an ally, the Bourbon king Ferdinand I and Queen Maria Carolina of the Two Sicilies, whom he had helped escape from a Jacobin-inspired revolution that had set up the republic lasting 144 days, and who had given Nelson the estate of Bronte on Sicily.† He was not cold-blooded, but saw his occasional acts of cruelty to be nothing more than doing his duty.

Nelson, who loathed Jacobinism, effectively agreed to the

-----

* The family of Commodore Caracciolo still considers Nelson to be a war criminal.
† If you helicopter over Bronte, it is noticeable how often lava flows from Mount Etna have devastated the area, so perhaps it was not as generous a gift as it might have seemed at first sight.

Neapolitan government's insistence that the rebels be treated as though they were mutineers at sea. The nearest analogy might be if some Bolsheviks had fallen into the hands of the czarist Whites during the Russian civil war, and the Whites' ally Winston Churchill had not striven to save them. Although it is no justification in law, it is worth pointing out that had the Neapolitan Jacobins won, they would almost certainly have shown the Neapolitan branch of the Bourbon family the same lack of mercy that their Parisian counterparts had to their French cousins.

At the end of Britain's short-lived Treaty of Amiens with France in May 1803, Nelson was appointed to command the Royal Navy in the Mediterranean, where he proceeded to blockade Toulon, not stepping off his flagship, HMS *Victory*, for more than ten days over the next two years. Meanwhile, Napoleon, who was crowned emperor of France in December 1804, amassed by far the greatest invasion threat to the United Kingdom between the Spanish Armada in 1588 and Hitler's Operation Sealion in 1940. It was in order to destroy the combined French and Spanish fleets that were expected to carry Napoleon's invasion force across the Channel that Nelson left England for what turned out to be the last time in the autumn of 1805.

One of those accompanying Nelson on his final journey from The George Hotel at Portsmouth to HMS *Victory* was someone called Admiral Sir Isaac Coffin. (Omens rarely come more blatant than that, except perhaps in the case of his distant kinsman Colonel Richard Pine-Coffin.) The poet Robert Southey witnessed Nelson's departure from Southsea beach. "A crowd collected," he recalled, "pressing forward to obtain sight of his face; many were in tears, and many knelt down before him, and blessed him as he passed. England has had many heroes, but never one who so entirely possessed the love of his fellow-countrymen."[15]

"I entreat, my dear Emma, that you will cheer up," Nelson wrote to Lady Hamilton on September 17, "and we will look forward to many, many happy years; and be surrounded by our children's children."[16] In fact, their illegitimate only child, Horatia, did go on to have ten children. Nelson looked forward to peace, but only one on British terms, having written the previous year: "I most sincerely hope that by the destruction of Buonaparte [sic] that war with all nations will cease."[17] It was one of the few times in his life that the admiral was being naïve.

On October 19, 1805, the French and Spanish combined fleet of thirty-three ships of the line suddenly left the safety of Cádiz harbor in southern Spain and attempted to pass through the Straits of Gibraltar. Nelson immediately gave chase with his twenty-seven ships of the line. Although outnumbered in ships, men, and guns, he put his trust in the superb fighting quality of his fleet and promised the Admiralty back in London that they could rely upon his every exertion "that as an Enemy's Fleet they may be annihilated."[18] *Annihilation* was a word he used often; it was what he ceaselessly looked for in battle and what sets him apart from many other commanders in history. Of course it was easier in naval than in military engagements, because ships sink with their entire crews on board, but nonetheless Nelson's hatred of the French and their Revolution was total and intimately bound up with its atheism, which, as the son of a clergyman, he could be expected to see in existential terms. (The duke of Wellington, by contrast, was a Francophile who had been schooled in France, spoke French, and became ambassador to Paris. His sole animus was against Napoleon personally.)

The dawn of Monday, October 21, 1805, was misty, but it gave way to fine weather a few hours later when the combined fleet was spotted from the topmost masts of HMS *Victory*, a few miles to the west of Cape Trafalgar off the coast of southwest Spain near Cádiz. Nelson summoned his captains and explained his battle plan, which was in essence to smash through the enemy's line in two columns, cutting it roughly into equal thirds, and then to concentrate the faster and more accurate British firepower on the rear two thirds, thus equaling up the numbers between the combined fleet and the Royal Navy. Edmond Jurien de la Gravière, the nineteenth-century French naval historian, wrote, *"Le genie de Nelson c'est d'avoir compris notre faiblesse."* ("The genius of Nelson was to have understood our weakness.") He was right; Nelson hoped to bring on the "pell-mell" battle that he believed would give him a chance to destroy more enemy ships than in traditional line-versus-line engagement. So he signaled the fleet to "form order of sailing in two columns." It was imaginative and daring, and his captains—he borrowed from Shakespeare to call them a band of brothers—later called it the "Nelson Touch."

The plan required tremendous skill and courage to implement, because the enemy would be able to fire broadsides into the British ships for an agonizingly long time before they could respond. Nelson led one column in *Victory,* and Vice Admiral Sir Cuthbert Collingwood, his second in command, the other in HMS *Royal Sovereign.* Another of his orders, "No captain can do very wrong if he places his ship alongside that of an enemy," has been wrongly interpreted as being contemptuous of Nelson's French and Spanish enemies, because it seemed to assume that if they were placed alongside each other, the Royal Navy would inevitably be victorious. In fact, it marked Nelson's concern that some of the ships at the tail ends of the two British columns would not get into close-quarter action with enough October daylight to ensure the crushing result he craved. It also recognized the superior rate of fire that the better-trained British gun crews had over their French and Spanish counterparts.

At 11:35 A.M., while the drums were beating the call to action, the gun ports were being raised, the cannons run out, and the decks sanded down to make them less slippery when the blood started to spurt, Nelson ordered his famous signal—"England expects that every man will do his duty"—to be hoisted from his flagship. He told Flag Lieutenant Pascoe that he hoped it would "amuse the fleet."[19] Whether it amused the sailors that day is unknown, but it has certainly inspired generations of his fellow countrymen.

He himself then set off, painfully slowly due to a weak wind, to engage no fewer than three French ships: the *Neptune, Bucentaure,* and *Redoutable.* Nelson's battle plan involved his captains keeping their composure and steadying their men and steering silently in line ahead taking broadside fire as they did so. To be on the receiving end of a full-scale broadside from a ship of the line was a truly terrible thing, but Collingwood coolly ate an apple as *Royal Sovereign* was being raked with fire, before he could return a shot. The battle went precisely according to Nelson's plan.

Under heavy fire from the *Bucentaure* and *Redoutable*, *Victory* managed to sail between them, pouring fire into each as she passed. *Bucentaure* was raked from helm to stern, and the 74-gun *Redoutable* was then rammed by *Victory*, swinging to starboard as the rigging of the two great ships locked together. Today we can scarcely comprehend the horror of a sea battle such as Trafalgar. For hour after hour, cannons fired 18-, 24-, and sometimes even 32-pound iron cannonballs that smashed into the wooden hulls of warships, sending long shards of timber and splinters flying around decks packed with men. The twenty-seven British ships of the line at Trafalgar had a total of 2,148 guns on board, many of them of much higher caliber than the 400 guns deployed on both sides at the Battle of Waterloo, which was fought in a far larger area.

The French and Spanish had 2,862 guns at the battle, so together there were more than 12 times more cannons at Trafalgar than at Waterloo. And they were kept even more busy. In four hours at Trafalgar, HMS *Victory* spent between 6 and 7 tons of gunpowder, firing 4,243 cannonballs and 371 double-headed grape- and case shot, and 4,000 musket balls. For those up on the top deck there was the ever-present terror of being raked with grapeshot. The firing of the Royal Marines stationed at the hammock nettings of HMS *Victory* was at point blank range, and any hope the French might have had of boarding her was destroyed by the murderous fire aimed at them by the 68-pound carronades firing grapeshot from her bow and stern. The British broadsides from below were fired at such short range that to miss was next to impossible. Yet the same was true of the French snipers stationed in *Redoutable*'s rigging.

Nelson had paid a guinea each for the four large, silver-embroidered stars of various orders of chivalry that were sewn onto his coat, plus twenty-five shillings for the Neapolitan order of St. Ferdinand. These made him conspicuous even at a distance. The place he chose to stand during the battle also meant that, as one of his biographers put it, "it did not take marksmanship to hit an admiral covered in stars at fifty feet."[20] He was almost inviting a sharpshooter's bullet as he sparkled away on the quarterdeck of HMS *Victory* that afternoon. The sniper's musket was charged with a lead ball that you can see today in the National Maritime Museum in Greenwich, measuring 0.59 inch in diameter and weighing 0.77 ounce. It hit Nelson in the shoulder, knocking him to the ground.

In the din of the battle, no one heard the shot, but its effect was devastating to both Nelson and Britain. The ball "struck Nelson high in the front of his left shoulder, piercing the epaulette and dragging pieces of gold lace and silk pad with it as it drove deep into his body." He suffered fractured ribs, a perforated lung, a spinal injury, and a ruptured artery, "but apparently made little complaint," merely stating "I felt it break my back."[21] To prevent the crew from becoming demoralized, a handkerchief was placed over his face so that no one could recognize him as he was taken belowdecks. Once there and lain down he told *Victory*'s Captain Hardy, "They have done for me at last. My backbone is shot through." The surgeon quickly ascertained that the admiral was correct, and there was nothing that could be done for him. It was a poignant, slow, painful death in the lantern-lit cockpit.

For another three hours, Nelson's life ebbed away as the battle continued. First the *Redoutable* surrendered, with 522 dead out of a complement of 643, then the Spanish flagship *Santísima Trinidad*. "I should have liked to have lived a little longer," he said. "Don't throw me overboard, Hardy," he added, and "Hardy, I believe they have done it at last." Before Nelson expired, however, Hardy was able to inform him that fourteen enemy ships had "struck" their colors—that is, surrendered—for the loss of not a single British vessel. Nelson, therefore, knew that he had won a truly extraordinary victory and would be remembered as one of the greatest admirals in history. Indeed, the final count was even better: twenty-two enemy ships were sunk or captured for no ship lost to the Royal Navy. Nelson's last words were sublime. "Thank God I have done my duty," he said, as he slipped into immortal glory.[22] The king shrewdly observed to Nelson's brother that it was precisely the death that Nelson would have wanted.

The victory at Trafalgar gave Britain a global naval dominance that it was to enjoy for the next hundred years, until the Germans started building their High Seas fleet before World War I. More immediately, it relieved any fears that Britons had that Napoleon could invade the home islands, however successful he might be on the Continent, fears that until then had been very real, to the point that mothers would scare their children into good behavior by the threat that otherwise "Boney might come." Britons did not know how they could win a land war against Napoleonic France, but they now knew they could not lose a naval one.

Thus when Nelson died at Trafalgar, the young poet Samuel Taylor Coleridge, who was in Italy at the time, found himself repeatedly accosted by Englishmen he did not know, with tears running down their (and his) cheeks. Benjamin West portrayed Nelson ascending into the arms of a deified Britannia. Dogs, carnations, streets, the tallest column in London, and a new strain of gooseberry were all named after him. He was a particularly English hero; when the Irish Republican Army wanted to make an anti-English protest to celebrate the fiftieth anniversary of the Easter Rising in 1966, they blew up the statue of Nelson in the middle of Dublin.

Nelson's funeral at St. Paul's Cathedral brought London to a halt; it had been a long time since anyone had inspired such popular adulation, and there was to be no such public outpouring of raw emotion until the death of Diana, princess of Wales, in 1997. Although eight admirals, all of them in tears, carried his coffin, such was his controversial status in the Admiralty because of his ceaseless self-promotion and occasional refusal to obey orders that eighteen other admirals refused to attend. (It was a male-only occasion from which both Lady Nelson and Lady Hamilton were excluded.) An unpublished firsthand account of the funeral stated how "on seeing the diminutive stature of the man it's surprising that the bullet was able to find its mark," and "In the middle of this really triumphal pomp he was laid to rest about the kings and the giants of the ages."

A grateful nation awarded Nelson's brother an earldom and the huge pension of £5,000 a year, a sum that continued to be paid annually to the family until 1947. His wife was taken care of in his will, but such was the custom of the day, not Emma. Although Nelson's last thoughts had been of his country and duty, his penultimate ones were of Emma. Like King Charles II on his deathbed who ordered "Let not poor Nellie starve"—of his mistress, Nell Gwyn—but who was ignored, no one did anything for Emma Hamilton, either. She died an alcoholic obese pauper in Calais in 1815. Neither man could mention his mistress in the will for propriety's sake, and no other family member had any interest in being generous.

The war leadership lessons we learn from Nelson are straightforward: Grasp the initiative and don't let the enemy wrest it back; break the rules and disobey orders if necessary; show extraordinary bravery leading from the front; practice for battle ceaselessly, as Nelson did in his two-year siege of Toulon, so that the men behave in combat as if it were second nature; loathe your enemy with a clear blue ideological flame; have a treasury back home prepared to finance the organization of fantastically expensive operations (it is estimated that in 1805 some 40 percent of Britain's entire national tax revenue was spent on the Royal Navy); take your lieutenants into your confidence and inspire them; and foster a reputation for berserk offensives that always keep the enemy on the defensive.

And what of those undoubted personality failings? "The vanity, the absurdly inflated *amour propre*, the love of flattery," believes the historian John Adamson, "were integral to the realization of Nelson's genius as a naval commander. Nelson the incorrigible show-off was part and parcel of Nelson the victor of Trafalgar." Dreadful husband, passionate lover, convinced Francophobe, and vain egotist, Nelson was also Britain's greatest hero who made his country impregnable from invasion for more than a century. Although he could not win the Napoleonic Wars, Nelson ensured that Britain did not lose them. Although Napoleon marched in triumph through almost all the great capital cities of Europe of the day—Madrid, Vienna, Warsaw, Berlin, Milan, Turin, Prague, Amsterdam, and Dresden, just as he did through Cairo and Moscow—Nelson guaranteed that he never marched through London. In Trafalgar Square today, Horatio Nelson stands atop a 160-foot column, but he stands even higher than that in the love and regard of his people. For he was, as his devoted Emma Hamilton put it so perfectly, "the guardian angel of England."

CHAPTER THREE

WINSTON CHURCHILL

1874–1965

I t is one of the great coincidences of history that on Friday, May 10, 1940, the day Adolf Hitler unleashed blitzkrieg on the West, Winston Churchill obeyed an instruction to attend King George VI at Buckingham Palace in London, where he was asked to become prime minister. Yet it *was* a coincidence, because he had been chosen as Neville Chamberlain's successor the previous afternoon, before the attack took place, and, therefore, without Hitler's knowing whom his ultimate British adversary would be.

The king noted of that fateful evening that Churchill "was full of fire and determination to carry out the duties of Prime Minister."[1] Then, in the car coming back from Buckingham Palace, Churchill's bodyguard Walter Thompson congratulated him, but said his task was enormous. "God alone knows how great it is," the new prime minister replied.[2] The third person Churchill spoke to about the job at the time was his wife, Clementine, to whom he said the next morning, "There is only one man who can turn me out and that is Hitler."[3] Years later he also told his doctor, "I could discipline the bloody business at last. I had no feeling of personal inadequacy, or anything of that sort."[4]

The reasons that Churchill had "no feeling of personal inadequacy" was that he was a Victorian aristocrat born when the British upper classes were at the apex of the largest empire the world had ever seen, and in his background, education, and military career he genuinely felt no reason to feel inadequate about anything. He had been born in the grandest palace in England—not excluding the royal ones—was the grandson of a duke and not at all the dunce he self-deprecatingly made himself out to be in his autobiography *My Early Life*. Furthermore, he had already held several of the great offices of state and knew that he could fill the premiership, too, a post he had wanted ever since he entered politics more than four decades earlier.

He had been the youngest home secretary in seventy years, the First Lord of the Admiralty who had mobilized the Royal Navy at the outbreak of the Great War, minister of munitions when it employed two and a half million people and was easily the largest civilian employer in the British empire, and a chancellor of the exchequer who had delivered five annual budgets. He was sixty-five when he became prime minister, three years older than the age at which civil servants retired, and had delivered well over a thousand speeches. As he also put it in his war memoirs, "I thought I knew a good deal about it all, and I was sure I should not fail. Therefore, although impatient for the morning, I slept soundly and had no need for cheering dreams. Facts are better than dreams."[5]

Before Churchill had even won his seat in Parliament at age twenty-five, he had already fought in 4 wars, published 5 books, written 215 newspaper and magazine articles, participated in the greatest cavalry charge in half a century, and made a daring escape from a prisoner-of-war camp. "At twenty-five he had fought in more continents than any soldier in history save Napoleon," a contemporary profile of him was to state, "and seen as many campaigns as any living general."[6]

Churchill's upbringing had, like Napoleon's, been consciously designed to produce someone who could lead men into battle. He had joined the officer training corps at school, had been required to learn the famous Harrow School songs, which were full of exhortations to patriotic deeds of valor, and then attended the Royal Military Academy at Sandhurst, whose whole ethos was to produce the kind of officer capable both of taking objectives under enemy fire and of planning and executing wider campaigns. As in Napoleon's day, there was a thin dividing line between the military and politics: Plenty of soldiers entered the House of Commons when Churchill sat in it. Indeed, Churchill's primary reason for joining the British Army was in order to make a name for himself through his bravery, which would allow him to woo a parliamentary constituency, as he did not have enough money to do so owing to his parents' improvidence and his father's early death.

Yet the other reason—indeed the key reason—that Churchill felt that he could "discipline the bloody business at last" and "had no feeling of personal inadequacy, or anything of that sort" was because he always believed that it was his destiny to one day save the British empire. As a sixteen-year-old schoolboy at Harrow, Churchill predicted to his friend Murland Evans:

> I can see vast changes coming over a now peaceful world, great upheavals, terrible struggles; wars such as one cannot imagine; and I tell you London will be in danger—London will be attacked and I shall be very prominent in the defence of London. . . . I see into the future. This country will be subjected, somehow, to a tremendous invasion, by what means I do not know, but I tell you I shall be in command of the defences of London and I shall save London and England from disaster. . . . Dreams of the future are blurred but the main objective is clear. I repeat—London will be in danger and in the high position I shall occupy, it will fall to me to save the capital and save the Empire.[7]

Churchill had mapped out precisely his destiny as a teenager and did not deviate from it until, aged sixty-five and considered by many—including Adolf Hitler—as a hopeless has-been, he came to power and walked with precisely the destiny that he had prescribed for himself half a century earlier.

It has long been assumed that it was his seemingly endless close brushes with death that made Churchill so certain that his destiny would protect him until such time as he could save London and England. For even if you strip out those very frequent near-death experiences during wars in which he deliberately put himself in danger, such as on the no fewer than thirty occasions when he ventured out into no-man's-land in the trenches of the Great War, there were any number of other instances in peacetime when it seemed unlikely that he would live long enough to fulfill his destiny.

He was born two months premature. He was involved in three car crashes and two plane crashes. He was concussed for days after jumping thirty feet off a bridge, was staying in part of a house that burned to the ground in the middle of the night, very nearly drowned in Lake Geneva, was stabbed as a schoolboy, and had four serious bouts of pneumonia as well as a series of heart attacks. In retrospect the lack of an assassination attempt on his life was a curious oversight in an otherwise very dangerous life. He complained to Clementine that he found it difficult to buy life insurance, but on this occasion it is hard to sympathize with him.

"Sometimes when she scowls most spitefully," Churchill wrote of the goddess Fortune, "she is preparing her most dazzling gifts."[8] Because he wrenched his shoulder jumping off the boat that took him to his first overseas official posting in India in 1896, for example—an injury that stayed with him for many years—he had to use his Mauser revolver rather than a sword during the famous charge of the 21st Lancers at the Battle of Omdurman two years later. This allowed him to shoot four Dervishes at point blank range, including one who was trying to chop at the hamstrings of his horse with a scimitar. Being unhorsed in that melee, where the Lancers were outnumbered by ten to one, meant almost certain death: The regiment suffered almost 25 percent casualties.

It was partly Churchill's extremely dangerous time on the Afghan-Pakistan border in 1896 and 1897, and in the Sudan in 1898, which had brought him up close to militant Islamic fundamentalism, that allowed him to spot the fanatical nature of Nazism that so many of his fellow politicians missed in the 1930s. Neville Chamberlain met Adolf Hitler three times, yet he utterly failed to notice the cold fanaticism of the Nazis and their creed, just seeing the Führer in classically British class terms as "the commonest little dog you ever saw."[9] Churchill never met Hitler, but having seen fanaticism in action earlier in his life, and remembering friends who had been butchered by Pashtun, Talib-ul-ilm, and Dervish tribesmen, he immediately spotted the same phenomenon in the Nazis.

The other essential feature in this was Churchill's philo-Semitism. One of the good things he inherited from his father, Lord Randolph Churchill, was that he was brought up to like, admire, and socialize with Jews, attitudes that were very unusual and different from those of the majority of the upper-class Victorians of his youth. Churchill, therefore, had an early warning mechanism that allowed him to recognize Hitler very early on as a malevolent force on the world scene. Clement Attlee said that in the House of Commons before the war, Churchill told him in tears about the plight of the Jews in Nazi Germany, and Churchill never failed to denounce it. That was emphatically not the stance of most British politicians—of both the left and right—in the House of Commons at the time. "Why is your chief so violent about the Jews?" Churchill asked Hitler's publicist Ernst (Putzi) Hanfstaengl when there was a chance of his meeting Hitler in Munich in 1932. "What is the sense of being against a man simply because of his birth? How can any man help how he is born?"[10] Unsurprisingly, the meeting did not take place.

Although Churchill believed in an almighty, the role of the Supreme Being in his theology seems to have been primarily to look after the safety of Winston Churchill. Churchill did not believe Jesus Christ was divine, although he did think of him as a very wise and charismatic rabbi, who gave mankind what Churchill called "the last word in ethics." In that sense, Churchill's belief system, which he himself called the Religion of Healthy-Mindedness, was theologically a lot closer to Judaism than to the Anglican Church into which he was born. He joked that he saw his relationship to the Church of England as like a flying buttress, in that he supported it but from the outside. His belief system, therefore, tended to augment and support his sense of a personal destiny, which was in turn so important in his leadership.

Another important element in his belief system was his admiration for the British empire, which he thought to be a worthy successor to the great empires of the past and the chief glory of the British people in his own time. In his great wartime speeches of both world wars, he made regular references to the fact that the British people were not fighting merely for themselves, but for the native peoples of what he saw as the wider British family overseas, and vice versa. Here, too, his senses of duty and destiny intermingled. He was profoundly conscious, especially during the Second World War, of how the struggle was weakening the empire and its chances of survival, and at the end of his life—when colonies were given their independence across Asia and Africa—he considered himself to have been a failure for not having defended the empire more successfully.

Other than his philo-Semitism—which was to turn into fully fledged Zionism long before the Balfour Declaration of 1917—Churchill received little that was commendable or worthwhile from his father, who despised him and undercut him at every opportunity. Indeed, the more his father was aloof and disdainful toward him, the more Churchill seems to have worshipped him. Lord Randolph's only other service to his son was to die at the age of forty-five, when Churchill was only twenty, allowing him to escape the stultifying influence of this mercurial, quick-witted, intellectually brilliant, unstable, controlling, and at times deeply unpleasant man. In a sense, Winston Churchill was striving to impress the shade of his missing father all his life, despite having received little from him but irritation and occasionally contempt.

Yet Churchill was to adopt his father's Tory Democrat politics, many of his mannerisms, and several of his enmities. He wrote his father's biography in two volumes, named his only son Randolph, and fantasized about meeting his father in a beautifully written essay titled "The Dream," which he penned in 1947. When Churchill was finally financially solvent—which did not happen until he was seventy-three years old—he bought racehorses and dressed the jockeys in his father's chocolate and pink racing colors.

"Solitary trees, if they grow at all, grow strong," Churchill wrote in his book *The River War*, "and a boy deprived of his father's care often develops, if he escapes the perils of youth, an independence and vigour of thought which may restore in after life the heavy loss of early days."[11] Churchill was ostensibly writing of the Sudanese spiritual leader, the Mahdi, in that passage, but as in an extraordinary number of his writings and speeches, and even his eulogies for his friends, there was a good deal of self-reference, too.

Although Churchill was in tears when he spoke to Attlee about the fate of the German Jews, it must be noted that he was extraordinarily lachrymose much of the time. Tears welled up easily in his eyes; indeed, he used his lachrymosity as a political weapon on occasion, underlining for audiences the fact that he was genuinely overwhelmed with emotion. He could not make himself cry at will, but he could let himself be overcome by tears relatively easily if the occasion was suitably emotional. Churchill cried in public on no fewer than fifty occasions during the Second World War, for example. "I blub an awful lot, you know," he told Anthony Montague Browne, his last private secretary. "You have to get used to it."[12] Montague Browne recalled that Churchill's tears could be brought on by "tales of heroism. . . . A noble dog struggling through the snow to his master would inspire tears. It was touching, I found it perfectly acceptable." Churchill considered his lachrymosity to be almost a medical condition, telling his doctor that he dated it to his defeat by forty-three votes in the St. George's, Westminster, by-election of 1924. Yet there were plenty of times that he cried before that. A more accurate diagnosis was that he was an emotional, sentimental Regency aristocrat in a way that predated the Victorian stiff upper lip. Every admiral carrying Horatio Nelson's coffin at St. Paul's Cathedral in 1806 was in tears, for example. When people watched Churchill cry they were not disconcerted—as one might be by the sight of a premier in tears today—but rather saw him as a leader who did not mind wearing his heart on his sleeve. During a visit to the London docklands during the Blitz in 1940, for example, Churchill's chief of staff General Hastings Ismay heard an old woman say, "You see, he really cares: he's crying."[13]

Another classic example of Fortune scowling at Churchill when in fact she was preparing a dazzling gift came when he arrived in South Africa in October 1899 and tried to get into the town of Ladysmith. He was unable to do this because by then the Boers had cut the rail link over the Tugela River and were about to lay siege to the town. Once again, Churchill had been fortunate in his misfortune, because had he got into Ladysmith he would have been incarcerated there until its liberation three months later, instead of following the path that was to make him famous, to the ambushed train, and his subsequent prison escape. (The casualty rate for British soldiers in that ambush was 34 percent, even higher than at Omdurman.)

Churchill found time and again in politics that Destiny, Luck, Chance, Fate, or Providence—he tended to use them interchangeably when writing about them, which he did a lot—worked in his favor, even when they seemed to be working against him. He lost the by-election at Oldham in 1899 only by a whisker, for example. Had there not been a mere 2 percent swing to the Liberals, he would have squeaked into the House of Commons, so he would not have gone to South Africa and had the opportunity for making not just a local or national reputation for himself, but a truly international one just five months later.

In March 1931, Churchill wrote an article in the *Strand Magazine* titled "If I Lived My Life Again," about all the twists his career had taken and how it might have gone otherwise. "If we look back on our past life," he wrote, "we shall see that one of its most usual experiences is that we have been helped by our mistakes and injured by our most sagacious decisions."[14] He concluded in that *Strand Magazine* article, "Let us reconcile ourselves to the mysterious rhythm of our destinies, such as they must be in this world of space and time. Let us treasure our joys but not bewail our sorrows. The glory of light cannot exist without its shadows. Life is a whole, and good and ill must be accepted together. The journey has been enjoyable and well worth making. Once."[15]

By 1939, Churchill was in that penumbra between older politician and elder statesman, but he had not given up his hopes for the premiership, however unlikely it must have seemed. His following in the Commons could be counted on the fingers of one hand, and even Clementine no longer believed he would become prime minister. But crucially, he himself never lost hope. As well as foresight, his sheer level of self-belief was an essential part of his leadership and was evident for decades before the war broke out. As with other leaders in this book, failure was merely seen as a temporary setback that needed to be learned from, and then put behind you as you push on through.

Writing to Clementine from the trenches of World War I at the lowest point of his life, after the catastrophe of the Dardanelles when he had proposed a military campaign in Turkey that had failed miserably, Churchill wrote one of the most profound sentences of his prodigious literary output of six million words—with eight million spoken—when he said, "I should have made nothing if I had not made mistakes."[16] One of the frustrations about trying to analyze Churchill is that he always analyzed himself far better.

When Churchill was finally made prime minister in May 1940, the British had lost the war—comprehensively, according to every metric—but there was a huge difference between losing a war and realizing that one has lost it. This was all the more true when the country was now being led by an aristocratic English romantic, an historian and novelist who lived in a world populated by Elizabeth I, Francis Drake, Admiral Nelson, the dukes of Marlborough and Wellington, and other heroes and heroines who had first survived and then triumphed over various recurring Continental tyrannies. Winston Churchill's primary duty in 1940 and 1941 was to prevent the British people from realizing that they had lost the war, and nobody did it better, not least because he utterly refused to accept the logic of the situation himself. The reasons he gave for optimism in his great speeches were barely credible, but in the end he was saved by Hitler's invasion of Russia and six months later by the German declaration of war against the United States of America.

Even some of the British defeats early in the war can be put down as being a case of Fortune's seeming to scowl spitefully even as she was preparing a dazzling gift. The most dazzling gift of World War II, the thing that killed 80 percent of all the Germans who died in battle during that conflict, was Hitler's invasion of Russia in June 1941. Operation Barbarossa could have taken place six weeks earlier, but Churchill had supported the Yugoslavian uprising in late March and sent an expeditionary force to Greece. The Greeks were forced to capitulate on April 23, 1940, yet although Churchill's support for the Yugoslavian coup and the intervention in Greece looked disastrous at the time, later on it seemed inspired, though not for any reason to do with British arms.

By August 1941, Churchill was telling his assistant private secretary, Jock Colville, that the Yugoslav coup "might well have played a vital part in the war," in that it caused Hitler "to bring back his panzer divisions from the north and postponed for six weeks the attack on Russia."[17] He was supported in this assertion after the war by the senior German staff officer General Günther Blumentritt, who stated that "the Balkan incident postponed the opening of the [Russian] campaign by five-and-a-half weeks," while another senior strategist, General Siegfried Westphal, put it at six.[18] Since the Germans were unable to reach Moscow until the autumn, when Russia's rainy season turned to a winter so cold that petrol froze and the Wehrmacht stalled outside the city, giving the Russians an opportunity for their counterattack in December, the iron law of unintended consequences had once more acted in Churchill's favor.

When a Tory MP criticized Churchill for taking the risk of visiting the front only six days after D-Day, Brendan Bracken, the minister of information and the prime minister's closest friend, gave a witty and impassioned reply, in which he said, "Neither the honourable and gallant Member nor anyone else can persuade the Prime Minister to wrap himself in cotton wool. He is the enemy of flocculence in thought, word or deed. Most humbly do I aver that, in years to come, a grateful and affectionate people will say that Winston Churchill was raised to leadership by destiny. Men of destiny have never counted risk."[19]

Many times in his life Churchill's failure to count risk had let him down. His inability to weigh risk and reward had often led him to disaster. But he learned from each mistake, which is truly the only thing that ultimately mattered. The Dardanelles catastrophe, for example, had taught him never to overrule the chiefs of staff during the whole of the Second World War. Meanwhile, those politicians who carefully weighed the risks and rewards recommended a path that, if we had followed it, might have led to the extinguishing of freedom—including in the United States—for centuries to come.

If Britain had fallen in 1940 and the Royal Navy—easily the most powerful navy in the world at the time—had been forced to join the German, Italian, and French navies, then the United States Navy could have done little to protect the eastern seaboard. The Americans could, therefore, not have entered the war, otherwise Miami, Charleston, Washington, DC, New York, Baltimore, and Boston would have been destroyed by naval bombardment. Instead of these nightmares' coming to pass, there was a man who, aged sixteen, said, "I shall be in command of the defences of London and I shall save London and England from disaster." This profound sense of destiny and capacity for war leadership meant that Winston Churchill was able to save not only London and England from disaster, but ultimately civilization itself.

CHAPTER FOUR

ADOLF HITLER

1889–1945

Any understanding of Adolf Hitler has to begin by ac-knowledging the fact that he was extravagantly admired and even worshipped by millions of normal people for more than a decade. Of course Leni Riefenstahl staged the camera angles and tracking shots for films like *Triumph of the Will*—in which hundreds of thousands of ordinary Germans were shown in transports of delight over their Führer—but no one suggests that the people she was filming were acting, like extras on a film set. It was really happening, and it went on for years. Hitler was accorded adoration to a degree seldom seen for any politician before or since.

Yet despite this prolonged hero worship by millions, which continued even after it was apparent that he was losing the most devastating war in human history, the focus of it all, Adolf Hitler, was himself a completely mediocre individual. Because he was the central figure of the first half of the twentieth century—perhaps even the emblematic individual of that terrible century of resentment, hatred, violence, and cruelty—one could be forgiven for assuming that he must be intrinsically interesting as a person. He simply was not. Physically unprepossessing; with a relatively high IQ but a mind that worked on extremely narrow tramlines; incapable of normal one-on-one human interaction on the basis of equality; uncomfortable in anything approaching debate or discussion; a terrible know-it-all, bore, and conspiracy theorist; absolutely no sense of humor; very little traveled, even in Europe—even when he dominated Europe—Adolf Hitler was a nullity as a human being. (He was also a vegetarian teetotal nonsmoker; maybe one or possibly two of those afflictions might be acceptable, but he had all three.) He had absolutely no sense of self-awareness; was immensely boastful (even worse than Mussolini); a bad prose stylist; and, as it turned out, a useless military strategist. Even as an orator, where he was successful when playing on the resentments of his people, it is easy now to spot the rhetorical gimmicks he used.

So why was this pathetic excuse for a human being—the kind of person you would pass in the street without noticing, rather than actively crossing the street to avoid—worshipped to distraction for well over a decade by the people of the most socially and scientifically advanced state in continental Europe, even as he deliberately plunged it into the second global war in a generation? And once that war had started, why did so many people follow him to the bitter end? Why, by their own admission, did so many generals who had visited him to tell him that the war was lost come away convinced by him and ready to make further efforts to try to win it?

Adolf Hitler was undoubtedly charismatic, but charisma is a harlot's trick. Babies are not born charismatic; one can choose to acquire charisma, and when you had geniuses of the talent of Joseph Goebbels in charge of propaganda, Albert Speer organizing the mass rallies and their architectural backdrops, and Leni Riefenstahl in charge of the lights, action, and cameras, it proved possible to turn this entirely mediocre man into a charismatic superstar, especially when he himself had been thinking carefully about how it could be done. He would use little ruses, such as staring into people's eyes without blinking, and never being photographed wearing spectacles or a bathing suit. His deliberate policy of not marrying Eva Braun until the day before his and her suicides was intended to increase his allure to German womanhood—he received thousands of love letters and proposals of marriage from Aryan *Mädchen* during his rule. The method he used in his speeches of gradually and imperceptibly increasing the tempo and volume as the oration went on, while shortening the words and sentences, created an excitement in his audience that contributed to his charisma. Above all, his totalitarian control of all news outlets in the Reich meant that he could be presented as a charismatic near deity continually for twelve years through the radio and newspapers. When a lie is told often enough, loudly enough, and without contradiction, it ultimately tends to be believed in the absence of obvious evidence to the contrary.

It certainly wasn't his writing ability that made Hitler so attractive to the German *Volk*. *Mein Kampf* is repetitive, discursive, and very heavy going, even more boring than *Das Kapital*. Hitler exposes himself in it as a poor man's Nietzsche without Nietzche's capacity for epigram, who tried to extend Darwinism into politics in a way that Darwin himself would have dismissed out of hand. The phraseology of *Mein Kampf* is such that there's hardly a memorable, quotable sentence in the entire book, which is astonishing considering its author's role in the twentieth century and that this was his central testament.

Fortunately, we know what Adolf Hitler was thinking privately during the central part of the war, as well as what he was willing to say publicly. Night after night at the Berghof at Berchtesgaden in Obersalzburg, and also at the Wolfsschanze (Wolf's Lair) in East Prussia, he would keep his guests and hangers-on up until the early hours of the morning with endless monologues, and from September 1941 to the end of 1942 it was all dutifully taken down by Martin Bormann, head of the Nazi Party chancellery, and transcribed after the war by the great British historian Hugh Trevor-Roper, under the title *Hitler's Table Talk*.

This book contains the Führer's theories and thoughts about everything imaginable. As they sat up there in the Bavarian Alps, as the logs burned in the gargantuan fireplaces in the vast hall-like dining rooms and drawing rooms, with their hideous art on the walls and with chairs placed yards away from one another, Hitler would talk and talk and everyone in the room would listen and nod and laugh deferentially on cue at his attempts at jokes. Nowhere in the 745 pages is anyone ever recorded as questioning, interrupting, or disagreeing with him— as he came out with one utterly weird idea after another.

Here, therefore, are some of Hitler's beliefs, taken from his own mouth, as vouchsafed to his adoring entourage, without addition or deletion by anyone, especially not Bormann, who clearly believed they were insights of surpassing genius worth saving for posterity.

"It is enough for a Czech to grow a mustache for anyone to see, from the way it droops, that his origin is Mongolian," Hitler stated in January 1942.[1] "It has been proved that a vegetarian diet—and particularly a diet of potato peelings and raw potatoes—will cure *beri-beri* within a week," he told his courtiers on another occasion of the severe thiamine deficiency disease then found in Africa.[2] He also believed he knew what dogs were thinking, saying that "when a dog looks in front of him in a vague fashion and with clouded eyes, one knows that images of the past are chasing each other through his memory."[3] Hitler also gave vent to dozens of curious antipathies, for example to the grass lawns found on English country estates, which for some reason he loathed.

"Like chamois, girls are rare in the mountains," he said of his native Austria. "I must say, I admire those lads who tramp for hours through the night, carrying a heavy ladder and running the risk of being badly bitten by the watchdog—or having a bucket of cold water thrown over them for their pains! . . . In Austria it is in Carinthia that these happy practices are most prevalent, and it is there one finds the loveliest maids!"⁴ He claimed that one of the reasons that he was so physically hardy was that his father kept bees, which often used to sting him. It wasn't unusual for his mother to take forty or fifty bee stings out of his father after he'd visited the hives, because his father refused to wear the protective gear and relied on smoking a cigar to protect him, despite ample daily evidence that it did not work.

A recurring feature of the Führer's table talk was grinding, unrelenting misogyny. The reason he preferred buffets to sit-down dinners was that in the latter, where there was *placement*, "one is afflicted the whole evening with the same female neighbour." He said he always preferred a stupid "kitchen-frau" to an intelligent woman. "Nobody like Wagner has had the luck to be entirely understood by a woman," he said.⁵ "A woman who loves her husband lives only for his sake."⁶ On another occasion he told his listeners, "I detest women who dabble in politics. And if their dabbling extends to military matters, it becomes utterly unendurable. In no local section of the Party has a woman ever had the right to hold even the smallest post."⁷

Women had only four roles in life as far as Hitler was concerned: motherhood, primary school teaching, charitable works, and interior decoration. "A man who shouts is not a handsome sight, but if it's a woman it's terribly shocking," he once said with staggering hypocrisy, considering the decibel levels his own speeches attained. "The more she uses her lungs the more strident her voice becomes."[8] On March 10, 1942, Hitler claimed that "man's universe is vast compared with that of woman. Man is taken up with his ideas, his preoccupations. . . . Woman's universe, on the other hand, is man. She sees nothing else, so to speak, and that's why she's capable of loving so deeply."[9] On the same evening he also said, "I never read a novel. That kind of reading annoys me."[10] It was not that as Reichschancellor he had no time to read novels, but the entire world of fiction, that is, of the human imagination, annoyed him.

There were also endless predictions, virtually none of which ever came to pass. "England and America will one day have a war with one another, which will be waged with the greatest hatred imaginable," he said. "One of the two countries will have to disappear." On another occasion: "It will be a German-British army that will chase the Americans from Iceland."[11] Hitler made many long-term predictions about the world over page after page of his table talk and got almost every single one of them wrong.

Virtually every conversation recorded by Bormann contains references to Jews, about whom he believed all the standard anti-Semitic tropes of course, but also several extra ones that are not to be found even in the *Protocols of the Elders of Zion*. "No beings have greater powers of resistance as regards adaptation to climate," Hitler claimed of Jews in April 1942. "Jews can prosper anywhere, even in Lapland and Siberia."[12] He was convinced that President Franklin D. Roosevelt was Jewish: "The completely negroid appearance of his wife is also a clear indication that she, too, is a half-caste," he said.[13] He particularly disliked Jewish philanthropists: "They become philanthropists," he complained in January 1942, "they endow foundations. When a Jew does that, the thing is particularly noticed—for it's known that they're dirty dogs. As a rule, it's the most rascally of them who do that sort of thing. And then you'll hear those poor Aryan boobies telling you: 'You see; there *are* good Jews!'"[14]

Hitler's hatred of Jews could not abide the clear archaeological fact that they had a long lineage in ancient Palestine, so he proclaimed a belief in "a disaster that completely destroyed a humanity which already possessed a higher degree of civilization. The fragments of our prehistory are perhaps only reproductions of objects belonging to a more distant past. . . . What is there to prove to us that the stone axe we rediscover was really an invention of those who used it? It seems to me more likely that this object is a *reproduction* in stone of an axe that previously existed in some other material."[15] He thought it was likely that "the civilization that existed before the disaster" flourished in the three quarters of the Earth covered by the oceans. Belief in Atlantis often goes hand in hand with nutty sci-fi beliefs, and sure enough the Führer had plenty of them, too.

"It's not impossible, in fact," he told his surely by now incredulous listeners, "that ten thousand years before our era there was a clash between the earth and the moon that gave the moon its present orbit. . . . One can imagine that, before this accident, man could live at any altitude—for the simple reason that he was not subject to the constraint of atmospheric pressure."[16] Any of his listeners with the barest smidgen of scientific knowledge must have known this to be tripe, but there is no indication that any wanted to risk a one-way trip to Dachau by contradicting him. It is the kind of thing that mentally disturbed people used to write in green ink to newspapers, along with their theories that the Vatican, CIA, and Bilderbergers were in a secret conspiracy to prevent the world from discovering what really happened in Roswell in 1947. The closest modern analogies to what Hitler was spouting night after night might be the ravings of Reverend Jim Jones in Guyana or David Koresh in Waco, except this man was in overall control of a modern industrial economy, the most powerful country in Europe with huge offensive military capacity.

Hitler's acolytes stayed up till the early hours of the morning, night after night, listening to all of this, only rarely saying anything during these endless solipsistic monologues, and then usually only to move the conversation on to another topic rather than to question anything he had said. In a democracy, if one's boss starts to tell you that he can read dogs' minds, that a higher civilization once existed in regions under the sea, that young men routinely wandered around Carinthia at night carrying ladders on the off-chance of being able to seduce local girls, that Jews cannot feel the cold, and that potato peelings can cure virulent tropical diseases, there are steps that can be taken to marginalize him. Yet in Nazi Germany one could only internalize the feeling that maybe this man's plan to invade Russia—the largest country in the world, a country twice the size of Europe—was not so brilliant after all. Some generals tried to blow him up in July 1944, of course, but no one in his entourage seems to have ever tried to contradict him or even ask for evidence to back up his ludicrous theories.

One of the reasons that Hitler's intellect was so mediocre, and prey to such moronic ideas and almost every conspiracy theory going, was that he would not take any notice of anything created by Jews. He ignored or denounced the product of centuries of civilization if it had been originally thought or written or painted or composed by Jews. The lacunae in his understanding and appreciation of history and culture were, therefore, vast.

He was also a terrible show-off. Obviously it is something of a prerequisite for fascist—or any—dictators to be monomaniacal, but Hitler's endless boasting was extraordinary even by those standards. Having no one to contradict him in his immediate circle meant that he could make outlandish claims about himself, always to his own vainglory. Of his schoolteachers he said: "I was not a model pupil, but none of them has forgotten me. What a proof of my character!" On another occasion: "I haven't been ill since I was sixteen," which he put down to his superior willpower and the fact that he wore lederhosen all year round as a child.[17] In pretty much all his anecdotes he came out on top, defeating everyone with his brilliance.

He only once came out badly from one of his own stories, and that was the one he told about the only time in his life he had ever been drunk. It was the night he received his school certificate, signifying that he had passed his exams. He and his friends drank a quart (that is, 2 pints or 0.94 liter) of wine and at dawn the next morning—after being waked by a milkmaid on her way to work—he found he had lost his certificate. "In the absentmindedness of intoxication," he recalled during World War II, "I had confused the precious parchment with lavatory paper." When he reached the school he found to his dismay that "my certificate had been brought back to the school, but torn into four pieces, and in a somewhat inglorious condition. . . . I was overwhelmed."[18] He was told off by his teacher and still felt embarrassed about the incident decades later. Yet even in this trivially sordid tale he somehow won out ultimately, boasting: "I made a promise to myself that I would never get drunk again, and I've kept my promise."

So why was this absurd, mediocre, boorish, self-regarding, physically unprepossessing excuse for an Aryan superman so popular for so long? There are a number of reasons: He was thought to be selfless, not personally corrupt. Many Germans believed the racial theory of their own superiority, hence the importance of the Nazis' explanation—the *Dolchstosslegende* (stab-in-the-back myth) by which the defeat of the German Army on the western front in 1918 was blamed on Jews, Communists, defeatists, aristocrats, and *Untermenschen* (subhumans) back home in Germany. The German people were longing for an excuse for their defeat on the western front that was not based on the truth—that their armies had been overwhelmed and categorically routed on the field of battle by the Allies in the late summer and fall of 1918. Any account—however implausible—that blamed others for the catastrophe would be a vindication for them, one that they clutched at psychologically, however irrational it sounded. By blaming everyone other than the German Army for the defeat, Hitler was fulfilling a profound craving for the German people—the *Volk*—that even they themselves did not appreciate they needed. It is the principal explanation for why such a lazy and essentially mediocre man was able to command the German people for so long. In that, and of course the efficiency of the German general staff before and during the Second World War, lies the reason why Hitler was able to achieve so many of his goals up to the fall of Stalingrad to the Soviets in February 1943. He tightened his grip on the strategic aspects of the war only when things were starting to go wrong, which was precisely the time that he ought to have given a longer rein to those commanders who understood far more about military strategy than he—career soldiers such as Gerd von Rundstedt, Erich von Manstein, Heinz Guderian, and Erwin Rommel.

In the 1930s, the right resented Jewish involvement in Berlin politics, and Hitler adopted the views and policies of the paramilitary Freikorps groups, which had many ideas—about anti-Semitism, the *Dolchstosslegende*, the use of the swastika, and the title Führer—that existed long before the Nazi Party. The Freikorps grew up after the defeat in 1918 as a result of the political and social dislocation of Germany, and were right-wing nationalist militias, to which several future Nazis, including Heinrich Himmler, Gregor Strasser, and Rudolf Höss, the commandant of Auschwitz, had all belonged. Hitler took much of his anti-Semitic, ultra-nationalistic, and revolutionary ideology from the Freikorps.

While still in the army, working as an intelligence agent in 1919, Hitler was ordered to infiltrate the Deutsche Arbeiterpartei (German Workers' Party), which soon afterward changed its name to the Nationalsozialistische Deutsche Arbeiterpartei (National Socialist German Workers' Party, or NSDAP, known as the Nazi Party). He became its fifty-fifth member and an effective public speaker for it, and quickly became enamored of its ideology, which closely mirrored the Freikorps' and which he began to shape himself. In July 1921, having recognized he had a talent for oratorical techniques that allowed him to play on the myriad resentments of defeated ex-soldiers, Hitler became its leader. The key moment for his rise, however, was the attempted Beer Hall Putsch of November 8–9, 1923, in which four policemen and sixteen Nazis were killed. A heroic myth was built up around the putsch, with anniversary reenactments, flags, relics, icons, the "Horst Wessel Song," and so on. The cryptoreligious imagery and icons were a deliberate attempt to form a movement in which Hitler was the prophet, but it needed a bible. Hitler's short and comfortable incarceration in Landsberg Prison gave him the ideal opportunity to hone the ideology and write *Mein Kampf*, which argued that "those who do not want to fight in this world of eternal struggle do not deserve to live."[19]

By May 1928 the Nazis were still getting only 2.6 percent of the vote. Hitler openly called for the destruction of thirty other political parties in the late 1920s, but no one took any notice. What propelled Hitler to power was something that Americans did in New York rather than anything he himself had failed to do in Munich. Because of the Wall Street crash, and the Great Depression that followed it, the German economy was subjected to another bout of hyperinflation, on top of the one that had devastated it earlier in the decade. Capitalism was thought to have failed, and as so often happens during periods of high unemployment, people turned to political parties of the extreme right and left. By 1932 the Nazis were the biggest political party in Germany. President Hindenburg had dismissively called Hitler the Bohemian corporal, but Hitler turned down his offer of becoming vice chancellor under the former general staff officer Franz von Papen. In January the following year, Hindenburg appointed Hitler chancellor, with Papen as his vice chancellor.

Despite being loved by the German people, Hitler never lost his hatred. Such adulation and success might in others have lessened their fury at the world, but not him. He defined his enemies carefully. Less than 1 percent of Germans were Jewish or Communist organizers or Social Democrat politicians. So the overwhelming majority of Germans were never at risk of arrest under the Nazis, at least not until the very final few months of the war, when ordinary Germans were shot in large numbers for defeatism. Furthermore, by concentrating adulation on the head of state for twelve years, rather than on the party itself, Dr. Goebbels's propaganda system had made it possible to despise Nazis yet admire Hitler. "If only the Führer knew" what was being done by his bad advisers was a common refrain, just as it had been said of the czars in Russia for many decades before the Revolution.

What few Germans knew, or could possibly guess from the propaganda put out by every organ of the media without fear of contradiction, was that their Führer was in fact extremely lazy. He often stayed communing with himself until lunchtime and encouraged competition among his ministers, preferring not to make decisions on domestic policy if they could be put off. After 1938 he stopped holding cabinet meetings altogether, and on occasion his private office would ask cabinet ministers not to give the Führer facts on a subject as he preferred to approach issues with his mind uncluttered by any detailed knowledge of the issues at hand.

There is very little evidence that ordinary Germans particularly wanted a war at any stage between 1933 and its outbreak in 1939, but plenty that they trusted him entirely to do what was best for them, and after resounding coups such as the remilitarization of the Rhineland in March 1936 this blind trust seemed justified. By May 1937 Hitler had decided on the need for a war against France: "My generals should want war, war, war."[20] When senior commanders did not agree with him, such as Generals Werner von Blomberg and Werner von Fritsch, he deftly replaced them with others who would go along with his revanchist, expansionist plans.

March 1938 saw the *Anschluss* with Austria, another coup of staggering proportions. The Nazis nicknamed it *Blumenkrieg* (the war of flowers) because of the red and white roses that were strewn before Hitler as he drove through Vienna by some of the two hundred thousand Austrians who welcomed him there. Not a shot was fired in Austria as that great and ancient state joined the Third Reich, except by those Jews who committed suicide sooner than flee. According to the retrospective referendum on *Anschluss*, undertaken under Nazi auspices, in which "*Nein*" voters could be identified by the authorities, 99.7 percent of Austrians supposedly voted "*Ja*." (Just to make sure there was no misinterpretation of what was expected, the "*Ja*" box was much larger on the ballot paper than the "*Nein*" one.)

Hitler offered Germans and Austrians an unusual but as it turned out heady combination of hope and hatred. To peoples who had seen defeat and then hyperinflation within a decade, it worked. They hardly needed total immersion in Nazi doctrine, but they got it anyhow. By the time the war broke out an eighteen-year-old German soldier had lived for six years—for the most conscious one third of his life, ever since he was twelve—under a regime of totalitarian indoctrination that was spelled out by Goebbels in meetings with newspaper editors in the phrase "The leadership is always right."

By the time of the fall of France in June 1940—which had happened largely because of General Erich von Manstein's brilliant surprise "sickle-cut maneuver" that took fast-moving mobile units through the mountainous Ardennes forest behind the French and British armies to the Channel coast the previous month—Hitler's chief of staff Wilhelm Keitel was describing the Führer as "the greatest warlord of all time."[21] The Wehrmacht had achieved in six weeks what their fathers and uncles had failed to in the four years between 1914 and 1918. Small wonder they thought themselves invincible, and their Führer infallible. He told his generals that the war was won, and all it now took was for the British to accept they had lost.

Of course Hitler loathed Churchill for his rallying of the British people, accusing him of being an alcoholic, unstable, and a puppet of the Jews. "Churchill is the very type of corrupt journalist," he told acolytes in February 1942. "There's no worse prostitute in politics. He's an utterly amoral, repulsive creature. I'm convinced he has a place of refuge ready beyond the Atlantic. In Canada he'd be beaten up. He'll go to his friends the Yankees."[22] It was extraordinary that a leader such as Hitler should have come to power at much the same time as ones such as Franklin Roosevelt and Winston Churchill, considering how completely different Hitler was from the other two. The key lay in the way that Churchill and Roosevelt continually attempted to appeal to the better angels of human nature—to honor, duty, sacrifice, fellow feeling, and so on.

Hitler told his generals about Operation Barbarossa as early as July 31, 1940, while the Battle of Britain was being fought and a full eleven months before he launched it. Nazi ideology rather than sound military strategy underlay it, as his generals ought to have spotted. The desire for *Lebensraum* (living space) for the German people in the east had been a dream of Hitler's since he wrote *Mein Kampf.* With more than half of European Jewry living in the USSR in 1941, he also had to invade the Soviet Union if he was going to annihilate the Jews. Finally, he would be able to have what Goebbels and other Nazis called a final reckoning with the Bolsheviks. Despite the fact that Hitler could have launched Barbarossa in 1942 or 1943, once Britain had been chased out of the Middle East (where 80 percent of her oil came from) or starved through an upgraded U-boat campaign, Hitler's restless ideological need encouraged him to launch the attack far too early. Yet hardly any of his generals balked at it.

Although his attack on Russia was premature, in another sense it was slightly too late. Because Hitler perceived a need to punish Yugoslavia and Greece for showing pro-British senti-ment in the spring of 1941, he lost six vital weeks subjugating those two countries, which would have been invaluable before the winter closed down the Battle of Moscow toward the end of the year. Nonetheless, the early successes of Barbarossa were stunning. The Wehrmacht covered two hundred miles in the opening week of the campaign, with Field Marshal Fedor von Bock's Army Group Centre capturing Minsk on July 9. On October 3, 1941, Hitler announced the defeat of the Red Army in a speech in the Berlin Sportpalast with the words "I can say that this enemy is already broken and will not rise again."[23]

Such hubris led Hitler to make a cardinal error, diverting large forces south from Operation Typhoon—the capture of Moscow—into Ukraine instead. Although he was to capture Kiev and Kharkov, these were minor victories compared with what the capture of Moscow would have achieved. When one adds his other terrible strategic errors—trying to capture the Caucasus and reach the Volga simultaneously; not retreating from Stalingrad once encirclement looked a possibility; attacking at the Battle of Kursk far too late and once the Soviets were fully prepared; falling for the Allies' deception during Operation Overlord and then not reacting fast enough once the truth became evident; allowing half a million men to be killed, wounded, or captured during Operation Bagration in July 1944; and so on—one realizes that quite apart from the overwhelming moral issue, Hitler did not deserve to win the war on grounds of military competence. Although of course his generals tried to blame Germany's defeat entirely on Hitler after his death, whereas they were often willing accomplices in it, it is clear from the transcriptions of the Führer's conferences that Hitler held a tight daily grip on all strategic aspects of the war from the moment that victory started to seem elusive in the late summer of 1942 until the end.

That Germany nevertheless conquered so much of Europe was a tribute to the capacities of the Wehrmacht. In less than eight weeks in the summer of 1942, it crossed more than five hundred miles in southeast Russia, reaching the Volga in August, which was a full fourteen hundred miles from Berlin. "No human being can remove us from this place," Hitler boasted on September 30.[24] He was wrong again, and in this case the human being's name was Marshal Georgy Zhukov, who commanded the Soviet southwestern front and coordinated the encirclement of Stalingrad.

Hitler's declaration of war against the United States on December 11, 1941, came partly as a result of his wild underestimation of American productive capacity, which is all the more extraordinary considering *Hitler's Second Book*, the sequel to *Mein Kampf* that he never published, in which he wrote extensively about the might of American industry. Moreover, the United States was uninvadable territory for the Wehrmacht. The sheer lack of a long-term strategy seems yet another schoolboy error in Hitler's *Weltanschauung* (worldview). "It goes without saying that we have no affinities with the Japanese," Hitler said in early 1942, yet only four days after Pearl Harbor he had thrown in his lot with them against the world's leading industrial power.[25]

The Holocaust must be counted as another economic and military error, as well as the foulest crime in the history of mankind. Holocaust deniers who quite correctly point out that there is no single document carrying Hitler's signature that authorized the Holocaust all too often and conveniently ignore that there are certainly words from his lips that do precisely that, again and again and again. At noon on October 21, 1941, Hitler said of the Jews to his entourage, "By exterminating this pest, we shall do humanity a service of which our soldiers can have no idea."[26] Four days later, speaking to SS Reichsführer Heinrich Himmler and SS Obergruppenführer Reinhard Heydrich, he said, "From the rostrum of the Reichstag I prophesied to Jewry that, in the event of the war's proving inevitable, the Jew would disappear from Europe. . . . It's not a bad idea, by the way, that public rumour attributes to us a plan to exterminate the Jews. Terror is a salutary thing."[27] Similarly, on December 18, 1941, at a meeting with Himmler, he ordered the systemization of the Holocaust. Hundreds of thousands of Jews had already been killed, but after that meeting the killing was to be industrialized. On February 22, 1942, Hitler added, "We shall regain our health only by eliminating the Jew."[28]

In wartime, therefore, Hitler deliberately embarked on the destruction of a well-educated and hardworking section of the German population at precisely the period when the number of Germans engaged in industrial production fell from thirty-nine million in 1939 to twenty-nine million in 1944. Hitler had been awarded one of his Iron Crosses by the Jewish adjutant of his Bavarian Reserve regiment in the Great War; he knew that Jews made fine soldiers. Yet he deliberately committed financial and military resources to exterminating the race that even a glance at the list of Nobel laureates should have told him Germany desperately needed in its existential struggle.

———

When Berlin was bombed, Hitler eschewed the Churchillian leadership technique of visiting the bomb sites to enthuse the local populace; instead, he drew the curtains of his Daimler-Benz and drove past the incontrovertible physical evidence of Hermann Goering's lies that no British bomb would fall on the capital. In November 1942 Hitler learned that the Sixth Army had been surrounded in Stalingrad, but he believed Goering's vainglorious boasting that he could resupply it from the air, just as two years earlier he had accepted Goering's assurances that the Luftwaffe could prevent the evacuation of the British Expeditionary Force from Dunkirk, without the need to commit the panzers. Hitler was a cynic in many ways, but for some unknown reason he kept believing Goering.

It is untrue to say that Hitler was constitutionally incapable of ordering strategic withdrawals. In 1944 three major ones were undertaken from the south of France, southeastern Europe, and western Latvia (the last by sea)—although not from Courland because he believed Admiral Karl Dönitz, who said the war could be won by a new kind of U-boat, which he needed to dock on the Courland coastline. But in late 1942 he sent out *Führerbefehlen* (Führer's orders) to Field Marshal Friedrich Paulus demanding no retreat at Stalingrad, and when Paulus surrendered on February 2, 1943, it ultimately cost the Axis a quarter of a million men. Hitler never spoke in public again, only on the radio and then very rarely, leaving public speaking to Goebbels instead. When Churchill was hardly ever off the radio for long, the Germans heard next to nothing from Hitler from the fall of Stalingrad until his final broadcast of January 1945, except for his 1944 speech after the failure of the July 20 plot, when he claimed his survival had been the work of "Providence."[29] In that last speech in January 1945, with the Red Army at the River Oder only forty miles away, he claimed he would win victory through his "unalterable will."

On March 19, 1945, Hitler issued his notorious *Führerbefehl* officially titled "Demolitions on Reich Territory" but known to history as the *Nerobefehl* (Nero Order). As early as January 1942 he had been saying, "If the German people lost its faith, if the German people were no longer inclined to give itself body and soul in order to survive—then the German people would have nothing to do but disappear!"[30] By early spring of 1945, Hitler gave orders for the destruction of Germany. He had become a Teutonophobe who wanted to destroy Germany because it had failed to live up to his expectations for it.

"All military transport and communication facilities, industrial establishments and supply depots," the order read, "as well as anything else of value within Reich territory, which could in any way be used by the enemy immediately or within the foreseeable future for the prosecution of the war, will be destroyed."[31] Thankfully, these terrible orders—which would have sent Germany back into much the same kind of preindustrial agrarian society that was envisioned by the Allies' momentary aberration known as the Morgenthau Plan of 1943—were ignored, principally by Albert Speer. (Similarly, the German general Dietrich von Choltitz the previous year had refused to blow up the Eiffel Tower.)

Down in the bunker below the Reichschancellery, Hitler meanwhile spent time with his vast model of what his home city of Linz would look like after his victory. (His parents' bodies were going to be disinterred from their graves and reinterred in an enormous bell tower.) The Hoover Institution Library and Archives at Stanford University has a copy of the marriage certificate for Hitler's wedding to his girlfriend, Eva Braun, at 4:00 P.M. on Sunday, April 29, 1945. Hitler's signature was smaller, shakier, and scratchier than on earlier documents, but Eva Braun's was bold and confident. This was the day her "Adi" was going to make an honest woman of her, after all.

Walter Wagner, the district marriage registrar, confirmed that "the persons mentioned under numbers 1 [Adolf Hitler] and 2 [Eva Braun] state that they are of pure Aryan descent and that they are not afflicted with inheritable diseases which would exclude them from marriage. . . . They also ask to accept an oral publication of the banns and to disregard all legal delays."[32] Wagner then asked, "Eva Braun, are you willing to take our Führer, Adolf Hitler, as your husband?" She most certainly was. They killed themselves just less than twenty-four hours later— at 3:30 P.M. on Monday, April 30, 1945.

Despite charisma's being something that people are able to manufacture—as with Hitler—we also know genuinely charismatic people in our own lives—teachers who inspired us, bosses who led us, truly remarkable people whom we would trust with our lives. Thank God such people do exist, because sometimes society depends upon them. Yet for all the huge effect Hitler had on the twentieth century, and for all the work put into trying to make him appear charismatic, Adolf Hitler was not such a person. His charisma was artificial and his personality that of a banal, soulless little weirdo with a lot of theories that today wouldn't have stood up to scrutiny in a single, serious half-hour radio or television interview. The deaths of seven million Germans, thirty-four million Allies, six million Jews, and so many others stemmed from the perverse ideas of one of life's utter mediocrities. The pity of it all is beyond description and explanation.

CHAPTER FIVE

JOSEPH STALIN

1878–1953

Any evaluation of Joseph Stalin as a war leader in the Great Patriotic War of 1941–45 needs to start long before it broke out. For Stalin's extraordinary personal toughness had been molded in numerous prisons decades before he had come to power; it is thought he killed his first victim as early as 1902, when he was twenty-four.

In the period before the German invasion of the Soviet Union on June 22, 1941, Stalin had been exiled for four years to a freezing and lonely Siberia; he had risked his life in the Russian underground fighting the czarist Okhrana secret police while Lenin and other Bolshevik leaders were safely plotting in Swiss libraries and cafés; he had played a dangerous and active supporting role in the October Revolution; he had overseen deliberate mass starvation policies at Czaritsyn (the city later called Stalingrad) on the River Volga during the Russian civil war; he had forced through the farm collectivization program that drove millions into exile, starvation, and death. He had organized show trials that led to the executions of hundreds of his Old Bolshevik comrades such as Grigory Zinoviev, Nikolai Bukharin, and Lev Kamenev on trumped-up treason charges; he gave orders for further mass starvation to crush the kulaks and Ukrainians (over four million dead); and perhaps above all he had murdered millions more in purges in which the victims' names were picked pretty much entirely at random in order to terrorize the entire population. This was the man whom Adolf Hitler decided to attack in Operation Barbarossa.

In his great comparative study of Hitler and Stalin, Alan Bullock describes Stalin's regime in the late 1930s by quoting the French revolutionary Pierre Vergniaud, "There is reason to fear that, like Saturn, the Revolution may devour each of its children in turn."[1] In Russia this was sometimes literally so. In his book *Stalin: The Court of the Red Tsar,* Simon Sebag Montefiore records occasions on which parents were forced to eat their own babies in the famines in Ukraine that the Bolsheviks engineered in the early 1930s in order to wipe out their class and ethnic enemies. In the Lubyanka prison in Moscow, he tells us, "many of the prisoners were beaten so hard that their eyes literally popped out of their heads. They were routinely beaten to death, which was registered as a heart attack."[2] Stalin even went so far as to pass a politburo resolution legalizing torture, though the Bolsheviks—astonishingly enough, like the Nazis—thought themselves decent, idealistic, even moralistic. Anyone who admires Arthur Koestler's masterpiece, *Darkness at Noon*, will immediately recognize the syndrome. (Stalin also saw himself as a poet, albeit of verses as seemingly unlikely as: "The pinkish bud has opened / Rushing to the pale-blue violet / And, stirred by a little breeze / The lily of the valley has bent over the grass.")[3]

Of the 1.5 million people Stalin ordered to be arrested in 1937 alone, more than 700,000 were shot. He loved to hear how his enemies died, as they were taken downstairs in the Lubyanka prison in Moscow to be executed in a purpose-built bunker. To roars of laughter from his entourage, his lieutenants would act out the pleadings of his victims as they begged for their lives just prior to receiving the bullet in the back of the head from the chief executioner, Vasily Blokhin. For some reason, both Winston Churchill and Franklin Roosevelt believed that they could somehow soften such a man as Stalin, or at the very least make him behave as other statesmen did.

The reason that Stalin was a monster was not only because he was an ambitious, cynical, cunning, murderous, vengeful, narcissistic, imperious, self-centered paranoiac—although he was indeed all of those things—but was intimately bound up with his devout Marxism-Leninism. "Nothing," writes Stephen Kotkin, Stalin's most recent biographer, "not the teenage girls, the violence, the camaraderie, diverted him from his life's mission."[4] The overriding driving force in his life was class warfare in its rawest state; his all-purpose remedy to all the ills of society was to conduct relentless merciless warfare against the bourgeoisie. Mastery of the ideology of the Communist Party of the Soviet Union, not just the apparatus, explains Stalin's long and exceptionally tight grip on power.

Stalin had embraced Marxism-Leninism as an adolescent while studying at the Tiflis Theological Seminary in the late 1890s. He declared himself an atheist and took on communism as his faith with all of the zeal (and ultimately the ruthlessness) of a convert. He refused to sit his final exams in May 1899, and by June 1907 his devotion to the Communist cause was such that he organized the spectacular robbery of 341,000 rubles (the modern equivalent of $3.6 million) from the Imperial Russian State Bank in central Tiflis, in which forty people were killed and fifty injured. It made headline news around the world. Although the Bolsheviks specifically outlawed such actions in their constitution, and Stalin, therefore, always officially denied involvement, it had been his heist, and after it he recognized an enhanced respect from his comrades.

We too often tend to ignore or at least downgrade the importance of ideology in Communist regimes because the lexicon is hard to decipher, the concepts and phraseology are fundamentally very boring and complex—indeed, they can make the theological controversies of seventeenth-century England seem fascinating and straightforward—and of course they bear no relation to the realities of everyday life as it is lived by millions of people. Yet to the Bolsheviks themselves, ideology was everything, and at the heart of it all was the class struggle. As Stalin put it in a speech in July 1928:

> It has never been seen and never will be seen that a dying class surrenders its positions voluntarily without attempting to organize resistance. . . . The advance towards socialism cannot but cause the exploiting elements to resist the advance, and the resistance of the exploiters cannot but lead to the inevitable sharpening of the class struggle.[5]

Nikita Khrushchev used to say that Stalin "was incorruptible and irreconcilable in class questions. It was one of his greatest qualities, and he was greatly respected for it."[6]

Part of Stalin's disastrous mismanagement of prewar Russian foreign policy, which allowed him completely to miss the buildup to Operation Barbarossa, lay in his total faith in Marxism-Leninism. He genuinely believed that there was little to choose between the capitalist countries of Germany, Italy, America, France, and Britain, despite the bacillus of fascism's having infected the first two but not the last three. Because under Marxist-Leninist thought capitalism inevitably leads to imperialism and thus fascism, Stalin was unable or unwilling intellectually to differentiate between the actions of Nazi Germany and the "bourgeois" West, leaving him open to be duped into the Molotov-Ribbentrop Pact of August 1939, which partitioned Poland and allowed Hitler a free hand in the West to crush France. Because his ideology declared wars between the capitalist powers to be endemic and something to be encouraged, he assumed that the pact would allow the Soviet Union to become what he called "the laughing third man in a fight," while the capitalist-imperialist powers destroyed each other.[7]

Within two years this woeful rigidity had left the USSR wide open to the largest invasion in the history of mankind, when Hitler unleashed more than three million soldiers across the borders of the Soviet Union, in more than 160 divisions. Russia was appallingly unprepared for the onslaught; the fortifications in the west of the country were still in the early stages of construction and the Red Army was stationed too far west. Illustrating his naïveté regarding Hitler, on the very day that the German invasion swept eastward, trains carrying oil and grain were going westward from Russia to Germany in fulfillment of the provisions of the Nazi-Soviet Pact. There is some irony in the fact that Stalin didn't trust anyone—except the least trustworthy man in the world, Adolf Hitler.

Stalin's refusal to accept that the Germans were going to attack, despite some eighty detailed warnings from Churchill and the Comintern's own spy networks—his spy Richard Sorge even gave him the correct day, June 22, 1941, for the invasion— meant that 80 percent of the Soviet air force was wiped out in the western regions before it even had a chance to get off the ground. The Russian armed forces weren't even fully mobilized after Hitler attacked, because Stalin did not want to be seen to be provoking him, despite the buildup over the previous months on Russia's borders.

In 1937 Stalin had moved against the one organization that he would later need most to defeat Germany—the Red Army—executing three of its five marshals, fifteen of its sixteen army commanders, sixty of the sixty-seven corps commanders, and all seventeen commissars. Marshal Mikhail Tukhachevsky was the model of the modernizing, thoughtful military reformer, but Stalin had him shot on trumped-up charges, along with tens of thousands of colonels and other officers whose loss he could ill afford four years later. Although the Red Army was the only institution of the state that could organize a coup against him, there is no indication whatever that it was planning to, and his purge of it was wildly overdone, given the darkening international situation. Stalin knew perfectly well that these Red Army officers were loyal to the Communist Party and that the treason charges against them were baseless. Some future marshals were imprisoned, tortured, but not shot, such as Konstantin Rokossovsky, who had his fingernails pulled out and several ribs broken during interrogations. When Stalin reappointed him to high command in 1941 he asked him where he had been, while knowing the answer perfectly well. Rokossovsky told his daughter that the reason that he always carried a revolver with him was so that he could never be arrested again.

In May 1926 the Soviet military rode on maneuvers on bicycles because they had so few tanks; in 1940 they had been effectively defeated by tiny Finland. After the Red Army massacres, it was small wonder that Russia was so unprepared for Hitler's invasion. The genesis of this disastrous policy can be seen in Stalin's idiotically isolationist speech to the 18th Party Congress in March 1939, in which he urged the Communist Party "to be cautious and not allow Soviet Russia to be drawn into conflicts by warmongers who were accustomed to have others pull the chestnuts out of the fire," i.e., the capitalist powers of the West.[8] Instead, right across the vast Russian empire Stalin created abattoirs for humans, supervising everything down to the best foliage to grow over the mass graves. "If only Stalin knew what was going on" was a frequent cry heard by Russians at each heartless new atrocity, yet Stalin knew precisely what was going on. It was he, or occasionally he and V. I. Molotov, his foreign minister, who drew up the lists for torture and execution, often entirely at random because it was the arbitrariness and the vast numbers that mattered in creating the Great Terror by which he ruled. The way that he was somehow personally absolved of the horrors was reminiscent of the way that many Germans similarly absolved Hitler of responsibility for his country's fate before 1945. The plain fact is that over a decade of relentless totalitarian propaganda glorifying the leader worked, in both Hitler's and Stalin's cases.

When he was told about the German invasion shortly after dawn on June 22, 1941, Stalin could not believe the news and said that it must have been due to a conspiracy in the Wehrmacht, adding that "Hitler surely doesn't know about it."[9] He ordered Molotov to ask Friedrich von Schulenburg, the German ambassador, for clarification. Marshals Semyon Timoshenko and Georgy Zhukov—both of whom had been kept in the dark about intelligence reports warning of Barbarossa— implored Stalin for permission to take immediate countermeasures, but even once Stalin had been informed that the German government had indeed officially declared war he still continued to stipulate that Soviet ground forces should not infringe German territorial integrity. (It was hardly a difficult instruction for the Russians to adhere to.) As Stalin's biographer Robert Service has written, "A military calamity had occurred on a scale unprecedented in the wars of the twentieth century."[10] The Germans penetrated hundreds of miles in days, captured three and a half million prisoners in a matter of weeks, and reached the outlying Moscow subway stations in less than four months.

Stalin was unable to focus his mind on anything on the morning of the invasion, and he let Molotov make the rallying address to the nation at noon. Visitor books and meeting agendas show Stalin hard at work consulting the military high command later that day, however, and a new high command, the Stavka, was established the next day, the twenty-third of June. Because of the military disasters taking place, Marshal Timoshenko was appointed its chairman by Stalin, who also refused the position of supreme commander de jure while of course retaining it de facto.

On June 29, 1941—one week into the invasion—Stalin suddenly disappeared from view and withdrew to his dacha outside

Moscow, not taking calls or giving orders, as the western front continued to collapse under the German onslaught. Was he doing what Ivan the Terrible had once done when he withdrew to a monastery, in order to underline his own indispensability? Or had he suffered a debilitating collapse in morale, or even a mental breakdown, as some historians have surmised? We cannot know; certainly Stalin never spoke of it later.

After four days, five key figures in the politburo and Stavka—Molotov, Georgy Malenkov, Marshal Kliment Voroshilov, Anastas Mikoyan, and the NKVD chief of secret police Lavrenti Beria—drove out to the dacha to find out what was going on. There they found Stalin slumped in an armchair. The way that he muttered "Why have you come?" implied to Mikoyan that Stalin feared that they were going to arrest him. Molotov said they needed a new State Committee of Defense to coordinate Russia's fightback. A suspicious Stalin asked who would chair it. Molotov proposed Stalin himself, which elicited the single word: "Good." From fearing a coup that would inevitably have cost him his life to being declared chairman of the key defense committee was a fine result for Stalin.

Thereafter Stalin operated a complex chain of command, principally made up of the Stavka, the politburo, and the State Committee of Defense, the last of which had dual military and civilian connections and frequently changing personnel. He consigned some key individuals—such as Russia's greatest soldier of the war, Marshal Zhukov—to operational and staff appointments in turn. His motive was to ensure that no one other than he should have an overall view of the war's progress, but he was also influenced by czarist military practice, which had a separate imperial and army staff, and the Leninist principle of the party always having the leading role in every aspect of society.

Stalin finally spoke to the nation on July 3, the first of only nine public wartime speeches that he delivered of any length. In this he was much more like Hitler—who gave only one public speech during the whole of the calendar year 1944—rather than Churchill, who made several hundred speeches during the war, and President Roosevelt, who delivered weekly fireside chats over the radio as well as States of the Union speeches in Congress and press conferences in the Oval Office. Nor did Stalin write in *Pravda* or the other newspapers, continuing his practice of never permitting his name to be attached to articles that he had not written himself. He did not authorize any new photographs of himself and was almost completely reclusive during the war except for the annual October Day parades at the Kremlin. This sense of mystique helped his image enormously. *Time* magazine made him its Man of the Year for both 1939 and 1942.

Stalin did not take over the chairmanship of the Stavka until August 8, 1941, by which time he had had the commander of the western front, Dmitri Pavlov, shot, although this time there was no show trial, torture, or forced confession. Voltaire had joked at the time of the execution of Admiral Byng that the British executed their commanders *"pour encourager les autres"* ("to encourage the others") but with Stalin it was literally true. Yet he could be just as harsh toward his own family. Stalin's son Yakov, a lieutenant in the 14th Armored Division, was captured near Vitebsk in July 1941, whereupon Stalin had Yakov's wife, Yulia, arrested and interrogated. Because all Russians had been ordered to fight to the death, anyone who had become a prisoner of war became legally a traitor to the Soviet Union, and their families were treated as "traitor-families," so Stalin was merely treating his son's family according to his own merciless rules, without favor. Later in the war he refused to exchange his son for Field Marshal Paulus, who had been captured at Stalingrad in February 1943, saying that he would not exchange a field marshal for a lieutenant, and in April 1943 Yakov was shot for refusing to obey a prison guard at the Sachsenhausen concentration camp, although there are other versions of how he died, too, including that he deliberately walked into an electric fence, a case of suicide by attempted escape. Yet Stalin was not heard denouncing Nazi brutality during the conflict. He knew this was war to the knife, in which horrific ill treatment of prisoners of war would be routine on both sides and the Geneva Convention completely ignored.

Stalin took relatively few strategic decisions during the war, but when he did overrule Zhukov and Timoshenko it tended to lead to larger Russian losses. He ordered Kiev to be defended to the last man in 1941, for example. "How can you even think of giving up Kiev to the enemy?" he said to Zhukov, the chief of staff, at one Stavka meeting, accusing him of speaking nonsense. "If you think the Chief of Staff can't talk anything but absolute nonsense," Zhukov bravely replied in the third person, "he's got no business here."[11] Kiev fell anyway, on September 19, after far more loss of life than was necessary. Robert Service is right when he says that in his refusal to contemplate strategic withdrawals, Stalin "acted like a military ignoramus just as he had been proved a diplomatic one in mid-1941."[12]

Most military historians believe that Russia could have won the war with far fewer than the 13 million servicemen's and -women's deaths that it was to suffer between 1941 and 1945. On July 28, 1941, Stalin signed Order No. 227, titled "Not a Step Backward!," which stated that any retreat without direct sanction from the Kremlin would be treated as treason and thus punishable by death. During the Battle of Stalingrad alone, some 13,500 Russian soldiers—almost an entire division—were shot by the NKVD for cowardice, even though men were sent into battle without rifles, being told to pick up those dropped by the men who had been killed in front of them. Yet it is worth considering whether such a war would have been won had Stalin, Zhukov, and the others not been such tough, utterly pitiless men who took little or no notice of the numbers of casualties. Stalin of course was inured to such numbers from his mass purges of the 1930s, and it may be that without such extreme sanctions, no one would have come forward to fight under such terrible conditions and against such odds.

After the Battle of Stalingrad was won—not least by Marshal Rokossovsky's successfully encircling the besieging forces in Operation Uranus in mid-November 1942—Stalin did not visit the city; indeed, he hardly ever left the Kremlin and his dacha, except to go to the Tehran and Yalta conferences. He never left the Soviet Union to attend Allied conferences except at Tehran in November 1943. As Marshal Biryunov recalled of the supreme commander, "Not once did his eyes behold a soldier in combat."[13] The closest he ever got was to within forty miles of the Minsk front in 1942, although *Pravda* entirely untruthfully reported him making key decisions on the front line there.

"Stalin himself was not the bravest of men," recalled Mikoyan, at least once Stalin was safely dead. Nikolai Voronov, commander of the Red Army artillery between 1941 and 1950, added, "I saw Stalin seldom in the first days of the war. He was depressed, nervous and off-balance. When he gave assignments, he demanded that they be completed in an unbelievably short time, without considering real possibilities. In the first weeks of the war, in my opinion, he misconceived the scale of the war, and the forces and equipment that could actually stop the advancing enemy on a front stretching from sea to sea."[14]

"The reality of war for him," as Robert Service writes of Stalin, "was his conversations with Zhukov, his inspection of maps and the orders he shouted down the telephone line at frightened politicians and commanders."[15] He was the ultimate coordinator, but he generally didn't interfere with military dispositions after it became clear that Zhukov and the other senior marshals knew better than the senior politicians what they were doing. He would set up debates in the Stavka between experts without letting on which side he supported, which is a sensible management technique whether you are a dictator or not. He certainly stimulated production impressively: In the last six months of 1942 the USSR built fifteen thousand aircraft and thirteen thousand tanks. The all-purpose Soviet T-34 tank wasn't as good as the panzers ranged against it, but the sheer numbers of them that were produced meant that it won the Battle of Kursk in July 1943. As Stalin is supposed to have once remarked, "In the end, enough quantity *becomes* quality."

Less applicable today was Stalin's other management technique of constantly threatening to shoot underlings. To Nikolai Baibakov, who was in charge of evacuating the Caucasian oil installations, he said, "Bear in mind that if you leave the Germans even one ton of oil, we'll shoot you. But if you destroy the installations prematurely and the Germans don't grab them and we're left without oil, we'll also shoot you." Baibakov somehow steered through this shooting range and died in 2008. When General Alexander Stepanov, the army commissar on the western front, suggested moving the staff headquarters eastward from Perkhushkovo in October 1941, the following conversation took place:

STALIN: Comrade Stepanov, find out whether your comrades have got spades.
STEPANOV: What's that, Comrade Stalin?
STALIN: Do the comrades have spades?

STEPANOV: Comrade Stalin, what kind of spades do you mean: the type used by sappers or some other?

STALIN: It doesn't matter which type.

STEPANOV: Comrade Stalin, they've got spades! But what shall they do with them?

STALIN: Comrade Stepanov, pass on to your comrades that they should take their spades and dig their own graves. . . . Stavka will remain in Moscow. And you are not moving from Perkhushkovo.[16]

Yet it was not true that the Stavka would necessarily stay in Moscow. On October 18, 1941, Stalin even had his personal train made ready to spirit him out of Moscow and go behind the Urals. If that had happened, and once it became known despite the official news blackout, the collapse in Russian morale might well have allowed the Wehrmacht to win the war in the east. Somehow, however, the Russians hung on in Moscow and also Leningrad, even though Leningrad was subjected to a grueling nine-hundred-day siege where there were incidents of cannibalism.

In 1997 the Finnish-based historian Albert Axell published a book titled *Stalin's War: Through the Eyes of His Commanders* for which he tape-recorded interviews with thirty of Stalin's surviving combat generals. "No excuses were accepted for slipshod work and penalties could be very severe," Axell wrote. "Stalin never forgave carelessness in work or failure to finish a job properly," recalled Marshal Aleksandr Vasilevsky, who had almost daily contact with Stalin during the war, "even if this happened with a highly indispensable worker without a previous blemish on his record."[17] Yet he would also look into the day-to-day problems of the army; when Marshal Kirill Maretsov told Stalin that his officers had nowhere to meet their wives and girlfriends for conjugal visits, Stalin had houses specially built for the purpose. Told that a bomb had fallen on the general staff's kitchens, Stalin ordered three sandwiches per person per day to be brought them in baskets. These kinds of small things were remembered by the generals, who were almost uniformly positive about Stalin's leadership even forty years after his death. (Of course they were hardly a statistically valid market sample, because they were the ones who had survived.)

Stalin's political decisions as a war leader were vital in strengthening Russian morale. He allowed an element of market economics to encourage peasants to sell vegetables to alleviate urban malnutrition; he permitted Anna Akhmatova's poems and Dmitri Shostakovich's *Seventh Symphony* to be broadcast; he dropped "The Internationale" as the national anthem for something more Russian and less cosmopolitan (which also contained a verse praising him); he met Acting Patriarch Sergei and opened Russian Orthodox churches after decades of imprisoning and killing priests; and he abolished the Comintern, the international Communist organization, while of course keeping iron control over foreign Communist parties by other means. Yet as soon as it was clear that Russia was going to win the war, he started to reimpose strict Marxism-Leninism; as early as 1942 it became illegal to praise American technology, for example.

Sir Frank Roberts, the British minister in Moscow between 1945 and 1947, wrote that "Roosevelt and Churchill were susceptible to Stalin because he did not fit the dictator stereotype of the time. He was not a demagogue; he did not strut in flamboyant uniforms. He was soft-spoken, well-organized, not without humour, he knew his brief—an agreeable façade concealing unknown horrors."[18] It was true that the marshal's uniform that Stalin wore every day was not flamboyant, but the horrors were not entirely unknown to Roosevelt and Churchill. The massacre of twenty-two thousand members of the Polish officer corps in the Katyn Forest in April and May 1940 grew out of Stalin's obsessive hatred of the Poles, at whose hands he had been humiliated in the Soviet-Polish War of 1920–21.

Once eastern Poland fell into Stalin's hands in October 1939 as a result of the Molotov-Ribbentrop Pact, the NKVD moved in to wipe out the Polish leadership and intelligentsia through incarceration and liquidation. In the Katyn Forest, Vasily Blokhin, Stalin's much-practiced executioner in chief, personally shot seven thousand Poles in twenty-eight days, so many that he had to wear a leather butcher's apron to protect his uniform from the blood and gloves because otherwise he would get blisters on his trigger finger. This won him a place in *The Guinness Book of Records* as the most prolific executioner in history. Once the Germans uncovered the corpses in 1943, first Churchill and then Roosevelt realized that Stalin was lying when he claimed the Poles had been massacred by the Nazis, a lie that the Russians admitted was untrue only in the year 1990. As Alan Bullock so comprehensively demonstrated in his *Hitler and Stalin: Parallel Lives*, the Nazis actually learned most of their repression techniques from the Bolsheviks.

Even though Stalin had wanted to preempt Hitler's attack at Kursk in July 1943, he allowed himself to be outvoted by Zhukov, Vasilevsky, and Aleksei Antonov at the Stavka—the correct decision, as it turned out. In that sense, Stalin's war leadership was closer to Churchill's than to that of Hitler, who did not allow himself to be outvoted by expert opinion. Stalin also released Zhukov to be battlefield commander at Kursk while nevertheless having the homes of Zhukov, the greatest of his marshals, as well as Marshals Kliment Voroshilov and Semyon Budyonny bugged by the NKVD. He also seriously considered having the second-best Russian general of the war—Marshal Ivan Konev—shot soon after Barbarossa. Stalin encouraged intense rivalry among his generals, and as soon as the war was over he humiliated even Zhukov when he sent him into internal exile by giving him the lowly command of the military district of Odessa. It was not possible in a totalitarian dictatorship for the dictator to share glory any more than power, because the two have throughout history always been so closely allied. Even though Zhukov had no interest in or intention of overshadowing Stalin, his very presence in Moscow would have had that effect.

Stalin used the smoke screen provided by the war to commit major acts of racial genocide, against the Poles, Balts, Molda-

vans, and Bessarabians, the Volga Germans, the Crimean Ta-
tars, the Chechens, and the Inguch. Just as this kind of terror
had not started with the war, neither did it end with it. Stalin
was planning a pogrom against Russian Jews, insinuating there
was a doctors' plot against him, when he fortuitously died in
March 1953.

"DEAR WINSTON," President Roosevelt wrote to Churchill
on March 18, 1942, "I know you will not mind my being bru-
tally frank with you when I tell you that I think that I can personally handle Stalin better than either your Foreign Office or
my State Department. Stalin hates the guts of all your top people. He thinks he likes me better, and I hope he will continue to
do so."[19] Proud of his ability to charm anybody, Roosevelt hoped
to win Stalin over to his vision of a postwar partnership between the two coming superpowers. Just over three hundred
letters were sent between Roosevelt and Stalin, the first from
Roosevelt soon after Hitler had invaded the Soviet Union, and
the 304th also by Roosevelt the day before he died in April
1945.

"When they are discussing American aid to the Soviet
Union," writes the historian Richard Overy of this correspondence, "they could be the managers of two large retail companies. Stalin's prose throughout is utilitarian, his letters much
briefer than Roosevelt's, occasionally mendacious but most of
the time simply economical with the truth."[20] Roosevelt wanted

to give Russia massive economic and military help through Lend-Lease and he wanted to create a lasting peace based on the four powers: Russia, the USA, Britain, and China. He hoped to create a close personal rapport with Stalin, albeit not one that could approximate the one he had with Churchill.

Stalin meanwhile wanted the Lend-Lease aid presented as a gift with no strings attached; he wanted a second front as soon as possible and an equal say in the postwar world with America and Britain (like Churchill he could not see the relevance of China at the time). He also wanted total Soviet domination of Eastern Europe, especially when it became clear that there would not be a Soviet-occupied zone in Italy.

From the start of their correspondence, Roosevelt wanted to meet Stalin, possibly in Iceland and preferably without Churchill's being present, so that he could establish a personal rapport. Instead, they first met at Tehran when Churchill was present, though Roosevelt and Stalin made teasing jokes at Churchill's expense, in front of him. It is possible to see the Tehran Conference of November 1943 as the moment in modern history when the USSR first became a major player in global rather than merely regional affairs, an achievement that must be properly accredited to Stalin.

Stalin's letters abound with his utter distrust of Roosevelt and the Americans. In 1944 and 1945, for example, he alleged that the U.S. Army was deliberately allowing the Germans to transfer troops against the Red Army; he insinuated that the Americans had given the Russians false intelligence on German plans; and he showed fury at any opposition to his plans to turn Poland into a satellite state. On December 27, 1944, he wrote to Roosevelt to complain that the Western Allies were effectively supporting Polish democrats, whom he characterized as "a criminal terrorist network against Soviet officers and soldiers on the territory of Poland: 'We cannot reconcile with such a situation when terrorists instigated by Polish emigrants kill in Poland soldiers and officers of the Red Army, lead a criminal fight against Soviet troops who are liberating Poland, and directly aid our enemies, whose allies they in fact are.'"[21] To describe Polish democrats as the allies of the Nazis shows Stalin's mentality at the time, only two months before Yalta.

Similarly, Stalin never really acknowledged the vital help given to his armies by the Royal Air Force and the United States Army Air Force. "As you are aware," Roosevelt wrote to Stalin in 1943, "we are already containing more than half the German Air Force in Western Europe and the Mediterranean."[22] Stalin was indeed aware but he was profoundly ungrateful; indeed, like Charles de Gaulle, he employed ingratitude as a weapon, believing, as he put it, that "gratitude is a dog's disease."[23] Neither man felt he had anything to be grateful for. De Gaulle thought his time in London served Churchill's and Roosevelt's purposes. Similarly, Stalin's Marxism-Leninism taught that if the capitalists accommodated the Soviet Union in anything at all it was solely because it was in their own interests—such as mollifying their domestic workers' militancy or opening up new markets. So nothing ever needed to be given them in return.

The constant *"Niet"* used by Maxim Litvinov, Molotov, and later Andrei Gromyko was thus an ideological as much as a diplomatic statement. As soon as any ambassadors seemed to be showing gratitude to Western powers, such as Ivan Maisky in London, they were recalled.

As both Churchill and Roosevelt hailed from their countries' aristocracy—the class that Stalin himself had largely succeeded in liquidating en masse inside Russia—and represented the bourgeoisie politically, Stalin was bound to perceive them as class enemies, because he saw absolutely everything through the prism of class warfare. Stalin told Marshal Tito that the only difference between Churchill and Roosevelt was that whereas Churchill would put his hand in your pocket to steal a kopeck—that is, one hundredth of a ruble—Roosevelt only bothered pickpocketing you for "larger coins." In fact it was Stalin who had his hands deep into Western pockets, whether it was for the five thousand aircraft or the seven thousand tanks or the fifty million pairs of boots that America provided to the Russians gratis, on top of millions of tons of aluminum and grain. The historian Antony Beevor points out the great irony, though one rarely acknowledged by Russian historians, that had it not been for the tens of thousands of Studebaker and Dodge trucks that Roosevelt gave Stalin with no strings attached, the Red Army could not have reached Berlin before the Americans in 1945.[24]

Nonetheless, Churchill and Roosevelt, and their successors Clement Attlee and Harry Truman, suffered from a profound sense of blood guilt vis-à-vis the Soviets. Whereas Britain lost 388,000 and America 295,000 killed in the war, the Russians lost a staggering 27 million soldiers and civilians, nearly forty times as many as the United Kingdom and the United States combined. Very often it had been Stalin's own strategy that had led to this huge number of deaths of course, but that did not lessen the sense of disparity felt by Western leaders.

Professor Kotkin is rightly at pains to point out that it was ideology rather than psychology that best explains Stalin's actions. Stalin probably was not even beaten by his drunken cobbler father in Gori, and the same seminary that so radicalized him also turned out soft Mensheviks. It was in fact his struggle as a Bolshevik and devout Marxist in the life-or-death struggles before, during, and after the October Revolution that truly molded him. "Stalin's marked personal traits," writes Kotkin, "which colored his momentous political decisions, emerged as a result of politics."[25] Even his most pronounced personality trait, his chronic paranoia, in Kotkin's correct estimation "closely mirrored the Bolshevik Revolution's inbuilt structural paranoia, the predicament of a Communist regime in an overwhelmingly capitalist world."

Stalin had once asked a victim about to be executed in 1937, "Can you explain your conduct by the fact that you have lost your faith?"[26] For Marxism-Leninism was a faith for him, one that was far more powerful than the Christian one he had been taught in his seminary. It took someone deeply imbued in Marxist-Leninist dialectic theology to be able to believe both that capitalist imperialism was in its death throes and that it also posed a mortal threat to the USSR. Indeed, Leninism stated that the closer to death that capitalism became, the more rather than less dangerous it would become, and Stalin believed it implicitly. His last book was about his belief that it was the historic destiny of Marxism-Leninism to establish a utopian society peopled by the New Socialist Man (who seems uncannily like Hitler's *Übermensch* Aryan superman).

Marxist-Leninist faith must carry much of the responsibility for the twenty-seven million Russians who died in the Great Patriotic War, on top of the untold millions more both before and after it. If Stalin had not been dictator of Russia in the 1930s its people and institutions would have been vastly stronger. Instead, Stalinism—which was not a perversion of communism, as modern Marxists try to argue, but rather the logical, final, and most highly developed stage of communism—gave Hitler his great opportunity.

CHAPTER SIX

GEORGE C. MARSHALL

1880–1959

On Tuesday, December 16, 1947, Winston Churchill's wife, Clementine, gave a dinner party in honor of the U.S. secretary of state, General George Catlett Marshall, who was in Britain for the Foreign Secretaries' Conference on Germany. The conference had opened the previous day, December 15, but had broken down almost immediately, over the Soviet government's demands for debilitating reparations against Germany. (The Soviets had shipped over half of Germany's heavy industrial plant to Russia in 1945, but that still was not enough for them.)

"The Conference had ended in dismal failure half an hour before," Clementine reported to her husband, "but Mr Marshall did not refer to it once."[1] Churchill himself was taking four weeks off from his work as leader of the opposition at the time, staying at the Hotel La Mamounia in Marrakech, where he was painting pictures and writing his war memoirs. Clementine continued, "He talked much about you and Mr Roosevelt with whom it seems he often disagreed and whom sometimes he did not consult. He said that he—the President—would direct his mind like a shaft of sunlight over one section of the whole subject to be considered, leaving everything else in outer darkness. He did not like his attention called to aspects he had not mastered or which from lack of time or disinclination he had disregarded. Mind you he did not actually use those words, but the gist and I thought much more were implied."[2]

Clementine was right and reporting Marshall accurately: He did sometimes fail to consult Roosevelt and certainly never slipped into the dangerous vortex of friendship with the president, as several other cabinet members and political cronies had, but instead always insisted on being called General rather than George. The first time he visited the president's home at Hyde Park, New York, was for Roosevelt's funeral. As a result of staying impeccably professional, Marshall had retained Roosevelt's respect from the day that he was inaugurated as army chief of staff—coincidentally on the same day that Hitler invaded Poland, September 1, 1939—until Roosevelt's death five and a half years later. He remained chief of staff until November 1945 and became secretary of state in January 1947.

At that dinner party, Marshall was abroad and among admirers and friends; he was relaxing immediately after the disastrous conclusion of the conference, a dangerous and depressing moment in the Cold War. He was reminiscing about the war as he and all the other surviving figures understandably did a great deal after that conflict, and of course he was speaking about someone who was dead and thus could not gainsay him, but who crucially never cowed him. He was possibly also changing the subject away from the demise of the conference. Churchill replied to Clementine eight days later, saying, "I am glad you had such an interesting dinner to meet General Marshall. I think we have made good friends with him. I have always had a great respect for his really outstanding qualities, if not as a strategist, as an organizer of armies, a statesman, and above all a man."[3]

If not as a strategist. Churchill's heavily qualified compliment to Marshall was of course a damning criticism of the grand strategy that Marshall wanted to be adopted for victory in World War II. The U.S. Army chief of staff needs to be a statesman and an organizer of armies, and much else besides, but he also primarily needs to be America's chief military strategist. There is no more important duty for a chief of staff than to formulate the strategy by which to win wars. So did George Marshall fail in that respect, as Churchill, Field Marshal Sir Alan Brooke (later Viscount Alanbrooke), and General Bernard Montgomery (Monty) all privately believed that he did? All three held this belief, because Marshall consistently advocated a return to German-occupied northwest Europe far earlier than they wanted to. Who was right?

Everyone, including Churchill, Brooke, and Monty, accepted that Marshall was superb at creating a massive army virtually from scratch; dealing with Congress, the media, and Presidents Roosevelt and Truman; sacking no fewer than sixteen divisional commanders; and much else besides. The only major question hanging over his reputation is about the timing of Operation Overlord, which Marshall initially wanted to take place as early as the fall of 1942 or failing that certainly in the calendar year 1943. In either year it would probably have led to disaster. Does that, therefore, mean that despite all his other undoubted talents, George Marshall was a bad strategist, and thus a bad chief of staff?

First, we should consider the fact that Marshall increased the U.S. armed forces by a factor of forty in only four years— from fewer than two hundred thousand to more than eight million soldiers in the U.S. Army: a truly extraordinary achievement. When the war began, the United States had the world's fourteenth-largest army, on a par with that of Romania. By the time it ended, it had sixteen million in uniform of one kind or another. In this process of vast expansion, Marshall had become so central to the American war effort that, despite having been a prime proponent of Operation Overlord ever since its inception, President Roosevelt told him, "I feel I could not sleep at night with you out of the country," and Dwight Eisenhower got the job of Supreme Allied Commander instead.[4]

If Marshall had lifted so much as an eyebrow over Roosevelt's decision, the job would undoubtedly have been his, and with it the fame and glory that today belong to Eisenhower, who instead became the public face of the U.S. Army, rallied the troops, and made the inspiring addresses. If Marshall had taken command of Overlord, the memorials, malls, medical centers, military bases, ships, trophies, golf clubs, mountains, schools and colleges, tunnels, monuments, camps, state parks, plazas, and boulevards and the executive office building adjacent to the White House presently named after Dwight Eisenhower would instead today be named after him. But he put his duty first, knowing that no one else could guide Congress, the press, General Douglas MacArthur out in the Pacific, Admiral Ernest J. King, the rebarbative U.S. Navy chief of staff, and the president himself in the way that he could—not even Eisenhower. Such an act of self-abnegation was a true mark of greatness. (In Britain it was mirrored by Alan Brooke, who also would have dearly loved to command an army in the field, but recognized that he needed to stay near Churchill in order to restrain him from ordering ill-advised adventures, in a way that any other chairman of the chiefs of staff might have failed to do.)

A graduate of the famed Virginia Military Institute, after serving in the Spanish-American War and the Philippines, Marshall had gone on to become an excellent director of training and planning for the U.S. 1st Division in World War I. He was involved in the planning of the highly successful forty-seven-day Meuse-Argonne offensive of September 1918, which ended with the Germans suing for an armistice in November 1918. He learned many important military lessons during this time and caught the eye of the commander of the American Expeditionary Force, General John "Black Jack" Pershing, who made him his aide-de-camp after Germany's defeat.

Of course the open warfare and high maneuverability of the armies in the summer and fall of 1918 were very different from the static trench warfare of the four years before the Americans had arrived in the spring of that year, so the lessons Marshall learned from the Great War also contrasted deeply with the ones that Churchill, Brooke, and Montgomery—whose experiences had comprised mainly static trench warfare—had taken away from the same conflict. (On visiting Ploegsteert in Belgium— "Plug Street" as the Tommies called it—one can see where Churchill was stationed for the first four months of 1916; the trench lines stayed totally static the entire time he was there. It is impossible to think of an active theater of World War II— even Monte Cassino—where the front lines didn't alter a jot for that length of time, except for during the siege of Leningrad.)

Marshall learned plenty of lessons aside from the strategic ones of course. He learned about what General Sir Ian Hamilton poetically called "the arctic loneliness of command," especially by watching Pershing. Years later, he recalled how Pershing had once leaned back in his car as he returned to his headquarters at Chaumont after a long tour of inspection, "and those who saw him took his attitude for discouragement. From that small incident the rumor spread that things were going very badly."[5] From that he deduced, as he told his wife, Katherine, in

World War II, that "I cannot allow myself to get angry, that would be fatal—it is too exhausting. My brain must be kept clear. I cannot afford to appear tired."[6]

It was astonishing that Marshall never did seem tired, considering his responsibilities, but he had a highly ordered mind, a talent for total concentration on the matter before him, a skill at delegating (once he had filleted the general staff of incompetents, leaving only his trusted lieutenants), and a redoubtable work ethic. This courtly Pennsylvanian gentleman with beautiful manners was incorruptible, single-minded, and astonishingly calm considering the pressures on him. Few were the times when he had to slam his fist down on the desk during Joint Chiefs of Staff meetings, but when he did his antagonist—usually Admiral Ernest J. King—never failed to back off.

Marshall's interwar years involved work so varied it could almost have been designed for a future chief of staff. He was a planner in the War Department; commanded the 15th Infantry Regiment in China for three years; taught at the Army War College; was commandant at Fort Benning, Georgia, where he proved himself a modernizer; commanded a large district of the Civilian Conservation Corps; and commanded the 5th Brigade of the 3rd Infantry Division in Washington State. In July 1938 he went back to the War Department as a planner and then became deputy chief of staff. Though he had actually not led troops in combat, he had had a wide and comprehensive grounding in many different aspects of military life before he was appointed over the heads of many other generals to the top post.

Marshall's first strategic decision after America entered the war was also his greatest, indeed perhaps the greatest act of world statesmanship in the twentieth century, besides Churchill's decision to fight on against the Nazis in 1940. Marshall and President Roosevelt together resisted the natural instincts of the American people to punish Japan immediately for Pearl Harbor, but instead put the defeat of Germany first. America's Germany First policy landed a quarter of a million Allied troops in North Africa within a year. The first American air raid from England against Germany was even earlier, on July 4, 1942. To take on the most powerful of one's enemies first, despite Hitler's not having provoked the war beyond declaring war on America four days after Pearl Harbor, was a farsighted act, even if Marshall was distinctly unhappy about precisely where or when in the West the first blow should fall.

Of course Marshall and Roosevelt had not come to the Germany First decision overnight; the War Department, with its hardworking, intelligent, and seasoned staff officers, had been war-gaming the various likely outcomes ever since Hitler had come to power. Men such as Leonard Gerow, Brehon Somervell, Joseph Stilwell, Albert C. Wedemeyer, Dwight D. Eisenhower, and several others had been discussing the best strategy to adopt, and even before the United States entered the war they had been discussing them with the British in the secret "ABC-1" talks held in Washington. The Clausewitzian view prevailed that the larger and more powerful enemy needed to be defeated first, and that was Germany, regardless of what had happened at Pearl Harbor.

Yet there the agreement ended, and severe disagreement began. For Marshall preferred a cross-Channel attack into northwest France as soon as the forces could be built up under what was code-named Operation Bolero. The Operation Torch landings in North Africa were, therefore, anathema to him and his planning staff. He didn't believe in encircling Germany under the peripheral strategy preferred by the British, which the Americans derided as a policy of "scatterization." Some of the more Anglophobic planners—of which there was no shortage—felt that the United States was being lured into the Mediterranean by the cynical, wily British imperialists, who needed to protect their bases there as well as their route through the Suez Canal to their Asian and Far Eastern colonies. (The South East Asia Command, SEAC, they caustically suggested stood for "Save England's Asian Colonies.") They were similarly suspicious that Churchill wanted to invade Italy not only to knock Hitler's ally Mussolini out of the war but also to open up further operations across the Adriatic into the Balkans, also apparently for selfish British ends. In spring 1942 in Washington, General Wedemeyer, one of Marshall's senior planners, quickly sensed that the British were up to something. As Marshall put it:

They seemed to have agreed in London to our planning concepts with their tongues in their cheeks. They continued to be unduly fecund with new ideas which hacked away at . . . the BOLERO plan. A sense of emergency would be associated with each effort on the part of the British to divert our resources and our men to other areas that held little promise of contributing to decisive results, but which would contribute to British prestige and greater security of the lines of communication connecting up their far-flung Empire.[7]

Wedemeyer wanted to "go for the jugular vein." Recalling a meeting of the British war cabinet on April 9, 1942, he wrote of an

initial joust with the British concerning definitive plans for a cross-Channel operation, for it was the forerunner of many discussions, with the Americans always keeping uppermost in mind the basic idea of concentrating and making a decisive effort against the heartland of the enemy. The British, on the other hand, kept returning to a concept of scatterization or periphery-pecking, with a view to wearing down the enemy, weakening him to a point which would permit almost unimpeded or undisputed invasion of Fortress Europe by our forces.[8]

Churchill, wrote Wedemeyer, "was a glorious leader and a magnificent English worthy with lamentable deficiencies as a strategist. . . . After 1941, the problem was to restrain the pseudo strategist in Churchill," Wedemeyer continued. "With their in-grained habit of assuming authority, born of centuries of domi-nation, the British naturally expected Washington to defer to whatever strategy was decided upon by their own military and civilian chiefs.[9]

"The defect of Churchill as a strategist for World War II was inherent in his islander's psychology. He held to the his-toric concept of Britain . . . relying on judicious statecraft, the Royal Navy, and limited military thrusts at fortuitously oppor-tune moments to win the day abroad. Then, too, he had been conditioned by his experience in World War I."[10] He blamed Churchill for not realizing that the era of fast armored vehicles, big bombers, and swift fighter planes had made the fighting style of World War I obsolete, a strange accusation to level at one of the fathers of both the tank and the RAF. Wedemeyer was on stronger ground when he argued that in the Mediterranean, and especially Italy, "there was no soft underbelly" and the lo-gistics were too long, whereas the cross-Channel attack taking Le Havre, Cherbourg, and Antwerp would be far easier, with afterward a war of maneuver.[11]

Marshall wanted the Allies to take the far more direct route to Berlin via northwest France, which he hoped would result in a gigantic Clausewitzian battle of the decisive kind that he had helped plan in the Meuse-Argonne region a quarter of a cen-tury earlier. Indeed, he supposedly erupted in what was de-scribed as a rare but awesome rage when he heard in the late spring of 1942 that Brooke and Churchill were not serious about an early invasion of Europe, which he thought they had agreed to in their meetings in London that April. He was sent that July to London to negotiate future strategy by FDR, who told him that "it is of the highest importance that U.S. ground troops be brought into action against the enemy in 1942."[12]

When Marshall discovered in London that the British chiefs of staff and prime minister were not about to support a second front in mainland Europe in 1942, thinking the Germans too strong and American troops too untried—and also that there were too few of them in Britain at that time—he threatened to swing the entirety of the American war effort toward a Japan First policy instead, directing 70 percent of America's resources there and only 30 percent toward Europe, rather than the situation under the Germany First policy, which was almost exactly vice versa. Admiral King, who had always supported Japan First, was delighted, but Marshall was surely bluffing over this. There were no advanced plans for any such thing, and crucially Marshall knew he did not have the president's support. Knowing this because of the prime minister's close communications with Roosevelt, Churchill and Brooke were able to call Marshall's bluff, and much the same thing happened the next year with the decision taken at the Casablanca Conference in January 1943 to attack Sicily that July. Marshall continued warning not to go into Italy after that because the terrain was a paradise for the defense and a nightmare for the offense, but he was overruled there, too.

It is difficult to work out precisely what was going through

Marshall's mind at these vital meetings and moments, because he was not given to introspection or diarizing, let alone to grandstanding or ex post facto self-justification. He had the Olympian self-confidence to feel responsible to his conscience and to God, not to public opinion or the media. Soldiers no less than politicians during World War II wrote memorandums with an eye to history, their memoirs and posterity, as much as to convey information at the time of writing. Many are the times in archives that I have felt conscious of some subtle attempted manipulation going on, that I am being spoken to as an historian rather than merely eavesdropping on the correspondence of others, especially when the situation on the ground seems to bear little relation to what is being described in the letters or memos. Working in George Marshall's archives at the Virginia Military Institute is not like that. He didn't write war memoirs and remained genuinely modest about his achievements in a way of which Montgomery, Mark Clark, and especially Louis Mountbatten were incapable, ultimately to the detriment of their reputations. As well as Mark Clark, generals whom Marshall chose for promotion included Jacob Devers, George Patton, Leslie McNair, Omar Bradley, and especially Dwight Eisenhower. He was a good picker of men.

When America entered the war, the former British chief of the imperial general staff, Field Marshal Sir John Dill, wrote from Washington to Brooke: "Never have I seen a country so utterly unprepared for war and so soft."[13] The British did not rate highly America's hastily raised conscript armies, their tactical doctrine, or their efficiency, and they didn't believe that the USAAF's belief in daylight bombing of German cities could lead to anything but a massacre of the aircrews. Churchill didn't share the British generals' doubts and pessimism, however. His extensive reading about the American Civil War convinced him that once the nation was fully engaged, extraordinary productive capacity would be unleashed as well as vast armies recruited, in a country moreover protected by its oceans from the kind of disruption suffered by British industry. He also believed implicitly in the courage of the average American fighting man.

Churchill was soon proved right. While in 1940 the U.S. produced less than half the amount of munitions produced by the UK, in 1941 it was two thirds, in 1942 twice as much, in 1943 nearly thrice, and in 1944 almost four times as much. In 1941 Britain had produced 59 percent of her maximum military output in the war, the United States only 12 percent. Overall, 13.4 million munitions workers in America produced four times more than the 7.8 million British. Whereas in 1942 one tenth of British munitions came from America, by 1943–44 it was over a quarter, and in certain important areas up to half. This meant that the American view of the grand strategy came to prevail by the time of the Washington Conference of May and June 1943 and that Marshall was able to impose his own time frame for Operation Overlord of May 1944, which in the event slipped only one month due to the lack of landing craft and one extra day because of bad weather. The British were fortunate that in both Marshall and Eisenhower they had two such good friends of Britain at the top of the U.S. military hierarchy. From early 1945 both men were ordering their respective staffs to go through their records deleting the more extreme anti-British statements—which suggests there must have been quite enough venom to worry them. Both men understood the problems of coalition warfare, so pertinently summed up by Churchill's phrase to Brooke that "there is only one thing worse than fighting with allies, and that is fighting without them!"[14] Churchill was quite capable of caustic remarks about the U.S. Joint Chiefs' strategy making, especially over the Operation Anvil attack in the south of France, which he abhorred. It was to that that he was referring when on July 6, 1944, he told his chief of staff and friend General Sir Hastings Lionel (Pug) Ismay that in their demand for withdrawing seven divisions from Italy for Anvil, "the Arnold*-King-Marshall combination is one of the stupidest teams ever seen." But he added that personally, "They are good fellows and there is no need to tell them this."[15]

Churchill was ultimately a better friend to Marshall even than was Eisenhower, whom Marshall had appointed to every senior position he had held from September 1939 onward. Like Marshall, Eisenhower had not commanded troops in action himself, and so had had no chance to distinguish himself on the battlefield—as he undoubtedly would have done if he had. He needed a patron in the War Department and found a ready

* Henry H. (Hap) Arnold was the commander of the U.S. Army Air Forces.

one in Marshall, who had himself been far from the most senior general available when FDR appointed him army chief of staff.

On June 14, 1951, during one of the least glorious episodes in American history, Senator Joseph McCarthy accused Marshall of having made common cause with Stalin in "a conspiracy on a scale so immense as to dwarf any previous such venture in the history of man. A conspiracy of infamy so black that, when it is finally exposed, its principals shall be forever deserving of the maledictions of all honest men." Two months later, Churchill published the fourth volume of his history of the Second World War, titled *The Hinge of Fate*, which included an account of the moment in June 1942 when he and Brooke had been in the Oval Office with Marshall and Roosevelt when the president had to break the terrible news to him of the fall of Tobruk. "Nothing could exceed the sympathy and chivalry of my two friends," Churchill wrote of Marshall and Roosevelt. "There were no reproaches; not an unkind word was spoken. 'What can we do to help?' said Roosevelt. I replied at once 'Give us as many Sherman tanks as you can spare, and ship them to the Middle East as quickly as possible.'[16] They were sent by Marshall immediately, thereby denuding the American army of them, as well as one hundred self-propelled guns, and those that got through to Egypt (after many were sunk on the way) played a large part in helping to win the Battle of El Alamein five months later. As Churchill wrote: "A friend in need is a friend indeed!"

In that volume and its two successors, published while McCarthy was keeping up his foul attacks on Marshall's honor and patriotism, Churchill lost no opportunity to praise Marshall—calling him, for example, "far-sighted and devoted." (Meanwhile, Eisenhower did not support Marshall; indeed, he cut a supportive paragraph out of a speech he intended to give in the 1952 election campaign.) Coming from the man who had opposed communism from the Russian Revolution onward, and who had tried to, in his words, "strangle Bolshevism in its cradle"—proposing to fight Lenin and Trotsky while McCarthy was still an eleven-year-old schoolboy—Churchill gave Marshall an invaluable endorsement, especially as Churchill had become prime minister again by then. In June 1953, during the Queen's coronation, while McCarthy was still attacking Marshall and even preparing to investigate the U.S. Army for un-American activities, Churchill stepped out of the procession up the nave of Westminster Abbey at the end of the service—thereby holding up the whole line of royalty, clergy, statesmen, and nobility—to stop to shake Marshall warmly by the hand. A friend in need was a friend indeed.

So what are we to make of Marshall's ceaseless advocacy for an early cross-Channel attack in 1942 and 1943, at a time when the Wehrmacht was still immensely powerful in the West and had not been defeated on the eastern front, the Luftwaffe had complete control of the skies over Normandy and the Pas de Calais, the U.S. Army had not been bloodied in battles such as Kasserine Pass, the U-boats were prowling undetected in the Atlantic, the Enigma naval code had not been successfully broken for the second time, and the Battle of the Atlantic won?

What are we to make of his demands for a major assault across the Channel before the Mulberry Harbors were ready, before the seas had been swept clear of German battleships like the *Bismarck* and the *Scharnhorst*, before the Pipeline Under the Ocean was built, before—most of all—there were more than a handful of American divisions in southern England to take part in it? Was Marshall deadly serious about wanting such an attack in 1942, regardless of the raid on Dieppe that August where 60 percent of the 6,086 men who made it ashore were killed wounded, or captured?

My strong suspicion—and it can only be a suspicion, because needless to say Marshall could hardly vouchsafe it to anyone— is that so talented a strategist as George Marshall, with his VMI education, Great War experience, and interwar senior staff experience, did not believe in a cross-Channel attack in the autumn of 1942 at all—but he did believe in keeping the British and his own president up to the mark, as well as keeping the Japan First lobby quiet. He knew perfectly well that he was going to be overruled by the British and FDR, perhaps for years, but that only by constantly promising to open a second front as soon as possible could the Soviets be encouraged to continue making the huge sacrifices and not pursue a separate peace. Above all, by pressing for an immediate cross-Channel attack, he could keep up the impetus in the War Department and the rest of the U.S. Army, Navy, Air Force, and Marines to a peak efficiency until the moment when American production and Russian successes in the east could finally overawe the

British and convince the president. Only by demanding an immediate clash against the Wehrmacht, which was undoubtedly still the best army in the world before 1944, could Marshall focus the energies of the Allies to properly prepare for one.

Marshall almost certainly knew that his bluff would be called in either 1942 or 1943. He controlled the timetable for how many U.S. troops arrived in Britain, without whom the operation could not take place in any case. He knew the vast amount of stores that needed to be shipped over, once the ocean was made safe through victory in the Battle of the Atlantic, which eventually was won in the summer of 1943. He knew Roosevelt's mind and the direction in which it was slowly turning.

Churchill and Brooke were thus wrong to denigrate his contribution as a strategist. Marshall was perfectly happy to look like the fire-eating proponent of the early offensive because he knew he would be outvoted by the British and his own president. Furthermore, he couldn't have cared less about the verdict of history on his strategic sense, because all that mattered to him was getting it right. If he had gone meekly along with the British refusal to cross the Channel in 1942 and 1943 rather than consistently opposing it, he would have found it far harder to nail them to the sticking post in 1944. When he did need to get his way—such as over Operation Anvil in August 1944 and in preventing Churchill from adopting a Balkans strategy that year—he had little problem in doing so.

George Marshall recognized as much as his fellow grand strategists that an overhasty return to the Continent could be a disaster that would set back victory in the West by years. He feigned disappointment, anger, and resentment in order to strengthen his hand as time went on, and in order to keep the Allies actively working toward Operation Overlord, which eventually took place at the right place at the right time and with the right strength, very largely as a result of Marshall's efforts. The man in the street, insofar as he has heard of George C. Marshall at all, knows of him only because of the postwar Marshall Plan, the economic salvation of Europe. In fact, he should be known for the plan to take Germany out of the war first, and afterward Japan.

Churchill did Marshall a grave disservice with his words "If not as a strategist" in that letter to Clementine, for Marshall was a key architect of the strategy that was adopted and was ultimately victorious. The armed forces he built have made the United States into the global superpower she is today, with all the benefits that have flowed from that for Western civilization. He should be a household name today, but fairness is not a feature of history. The fact that George Marshall was personally oblivious to fame is not a small part of his enduring greatness.

CHAPTER SEVEN

CHARLES DE GAULLE

1890–1970

When the British historian Philip Ziegler was writing his official biography of Admiral Lord Mountbatten, the supremo of the South East Asia Command in World War II, he felt compelled to place a notice on his desk that read "Remember he was a Great Man." Mountbatten indulged in so many acts of petty self-glorification that Ziegler had to remind himself constantly that, beneath all the showmanship and self-promotion, there was indeed a serious and substantial leader. Charles de Gaulle was also undoubtedly a great man, despite his deep antipathy for the Anglo-Saxons, which led him to acts of pettiness that demean him in the light of history. In the case of Winston Churchill and Franklin Roosevelt, de Gaulle's antipathy was entirely and enthusiastically reciprocated.

Great wartime leaders are often deeply influenced in their later thinking by major political events that happened in their youth. For Charles de Gaulle the crystallizing event was France's humiliation at the hands of Britain in the Fashoda incident of 1898, which, although it took place during the month of his eighth birthday, he heard about constantly during his teenage years because his father, a northern French minor aristocrat and nationalist, regularly referred to it with burning resentment. French expansion in North Africa along an east-west axis had been halted and rebuffed—bloodlessly—at the tiny village of Fashoda in Sudan by a more powerful British force under the command of Lord Herbert Kitchener, something that de Gaulle *père* never forgot nor forgave.

Charles de Gaulle's wartime Anglophobia—when he was living in London as a guest of the British after the fall of France—has been explained by his biographer Jean Lacouture in terms of "his childhood [which] had been marked by the sound of the word Fashoda uttered around him," but also by several other influences, including "because [as his second language] he spoke not English but German; because he had not thought much of the conduct of the British during the 1914–18 war, and because he was accustomed to a right-wing press—including *L'Action française*—in which all the misfortunes of French diplomacy were put down to the intrigues of perfidious Albion . . . because he blamed Lord Runciman and Chamberlain for the withdrawal at Munich; and lastly because he thought that Britain's military support of France [from September 1939 to June 1940] had been derisory."[1]

———

Part of de Gaulle's fascinating, infuriating personality was derived from his family background, part from his highly chauvinistic reading of French history, part from his army cadetship at the St. Cyr military academy, and part from the humiliations that France underwent at the hands of Germany between 1870 and 1944. One might take issue with some of de Gaulle's views—it had not been the British Army that mutinied in the trenches in 1917, for example, but the French—but instead of investigating the origins of de Gaulle's lifelong prejudice, it is important to place it in the context of his war leadership. For his prejudice against Churchill and the British, which was wholly matched by his resentment against Franklin Roosevelt and the Americans, was actually an important prerequisite for General de Gaulle's success, and was primarily what differentiated his from the other free European governments in wartime London.

For how else was de Gaulle to ensure that France was treated differently after victory was won from, say, Italy, which also fought on both sides in the conflict and was also occupied by both the Axis and the Allies? Instead of suffering the fate of Italy, in 1945 France was given a zone of Berlin to occupy, secured a Security Council seat on the United Nations, and was treated as one of the victorious powers, even though Italy had changed sides in September 1943, whereas the bulk of Frenchmen did not rise up against the Nazis for a further nine months.

The reason for the different treatment was largely the sheer truculence of Charles de Gaulle, who constantly demanded parity of esteem for his country with Britain and the United

States, and his success in creating a myth that supported that. He did not just bite the hands that fed him, he made them his hors d'oeuvres, entrées, and puddings. But he had to: It was the only way he could show he had teeth. In the words of his biographer Julian Jackson, de Gaulle achieved his diplomatic successes for the Free French movement almost single-handedly through the constant deployment of ingratitude, intransigence, "ferocious sarcasm," and "volcanic eruptions of contempt."[2]

De Gaulle's contradictions are an essential part of his myth: "He was a soldier who spent much of his career in opposition to the army, a conservative who embraced change, and a man of overweening ambition who twice renounced power voluntarily."[3] One might also add that he was an imperialist who withdrew from Algeria, a fiscal conservative who nationalized banks, and a French patriot who nevertheless envisaged the army invading metropolitan France from Algeria in order to make himself president in 1958.

It helped that Charles de Gaulle knew no fear, something he proved again and again. He was so brave in World War I—in which he was thrice wounded and made five escape attempts from prisoner-of-war camps—that he was pronounced missing, presumed dead on two occasions, and thus had the enormously gratifying experience of reading his own obituaries—which paid high tribute to him—not once but twice. His physical courage was legendary: There were no fewer than fourteen postwar assassination attempts on him, but after one, which came closest to success, in August 1962, he dismissively told his trembling prime minister Georges Pompidou, "Those people shoot like pigs!"[4]

Another attractive aspect to his personality was his love for his family, especially his daughter Anne, who was disabled. At her funeral in 1948, after she had died at the age of twenty, de Gaulle stayed at the graveside at Colombey-les-Deux-Églises with his wife, Yvonne, for a long time before leading her away with the words, "Come. Now she is like the others."[5]

"When the French fight for Mankind, they are wonderful," wrote André Malraux; "when they fight for themselves, they are nothing."[6] In 1940 they were fighting for the West, but having lost 90,000 men killed, 250,000 wounded, and 1.9 million captured in six weeks, they gave up the fight. In the interwar years de Gaulle had predicted that advanced tank tactics and blitzkrieg would deliver future victories, but no one listened to him. On the same day that Marshal Pétain decided to surrender to Germany, the junior war minister in the outgoing administration resolved not to.

For a Frenchman to leave France possibly forever is a terrible wrench, and de Gaulle was to be condemned to death in absentia. Yet on the morning of Monday, June 17, 1940, he flew into the pages of history when he took off from Mérignac Airport in a tiny biplane sent by Churchill, with only two bags to his name and one hundred thousand francs given him by Paul Reynaud, the outgoing prime minister. He landed at Heston Aerodrome, just outside London, at 12:30 P.M. Despite being only a junior minister in Reynaud's government, de Gaulle was the most senior figure willing to leave France and defy Pétain, and thus fully merited Churchill's foresight in aiding his escape.

The very next day—Tuesday, June 18—he broadcast the speech on the BBC that won him untarnishable glory. After frankly admitting that the Germans' tactics had "submerged" France and that the French government was in the process of capitulation, he said,

> Must hope vanish? Is the defeat final? No. . . . France is not alone! She is not alone! She has an immense Empire behind her. . . . This war is not confined to the unhappy territory of our country. This war has not been decided by the Battle of France. This war is a worldwide war. . . . I, General de Gaulle, now in London, call upon the French officers and soldiers who are on British soil . . . to get into contact with me. Whatever happens, the flame of French resistance must not and shall not go out.[7]

Very few people heard the speech at the time, but millions were to read it, as the French press was not yet censored. Suddenly the name of this junior minister of whom most Frenchmen had not then heard—a name reminiscent of the ancient Gauls who fought the invading Romans—represented the spirit of resistance to the Nazis.

De Gaulle had to work fast if he was to establish the Free French as an ally that could make a significant contribution to the eventual victory. He had to create a functioning provisional government for a country that already had a functioning actual government based in Vichy, raise money, found an army, a navy, and if possible an air force from scratch, agree a military strategy for the eventual liberation of his country, negotiate the constitutional future of the French empire in Africa and Asia as it was progressively liberated from Vichy rule, and deal with any number of issues that promised clashes with the British Foreign Office and American State Department. He did all this with a certainty in ultimate victory, and the restoration of French national honor and prestige, that equated with Churchill's own belief in Britain. Theodore Roosevelt's daughter once said that her father did not get on with Churchill because the men were too much alike; the same might have been said of Churchill and de Gaulle when it came to pride in their countries.

In London, de Gaulle was hampered by the fact that many more Frenchmen fought for Vichy than for the Free French, so the years 1940–44 were hard ones for him and the relatively small numbers of Free Frenchmen who heeded his call. Furthermore, within three weeks of de Gaulle's landing in London, Churchill ordered the sinking of the French fleet at Oran. De Gaulle characterized that action as "one of those dark bursts by which the repressed instinct of this people smashes all barriers."[8] Almost thirteen hundred French sailors were killed in ten minutes, for the loss of no Britons, in what has correctly been described as the twentieth century's most one-sided naval engagement.

Although some in the Royal Navy—generally the officers— had qualms about what had happened, Winston Churchill was cheered by a House of Commons relieved that France's mighty navy, the fourth largest in the world, could not now fall into German hands and be used to help invade Britain. It was the first time Churchill had raised a big cheer in his premiership. It was also the moment when the Americans recognized that Britain had the will and the necessary ruthlessness to fight on.

The military adventure in which de Gaulle's Free French, along with a British force, attempted to capture Dakar, the pro-Vichy capital of Senegal, was a disaster. It was code-named Operation Menace, but determined Vichy resistance easily repulsed de Gaulle's anything but menacing attack. "We went to Dakar with General de Gaulle" went the chorus of a song sung by drunken Royal Marines on the way back home, "We sailed round in circles and did bugger all!"[9] The way that Free French officers had toasted "*À Dakar!*" in French restaurants in London before they left made the British security services severely doubtful about sharing intelligence with de Gaulle, which was to become a serious bone of contention later on in the war; indeed, he was told about the plans for Operation Overlord only on D-2 (D-Day minus two), a mere forty-eight hours before it was launched.

Adjectives used to describe de Gaulle during this period include *truculent, aloof, temperamental, brusque, cold, reserved, rude,* and *gnomically ambiguous*—and that is in a sympathetic biography—and all of these attributes can be seen in his relations with his host Winston Churchill during the Second World War.[10] Equally, de Gaulle viewed the British as "cold, ruthless and duplicitous."[11] His insistence on being treated as a world leader of equal import as Churchill and Roosevelt was of course absurd when it came to their relative contribution to the war effort in terms of men and materiel. When the British empire contributed more than 15 million soldiers to the Allied cause and the USA had 16.5 million men and women in uniform by 1945, the Free French forces were only ever measured in tens of thousands, and sometimes less than that.

De Gaulle's insistence on parity of esteem frustrated "les Anglo-Saxons" to the extent that after Operation Torch in North Africa in November 1942, which had been conducted against Vichy France rather than the Germans, Roosevelt actively promoted the French general Henri Giraud, who had escaped from a prisoner-of-war camp and made it to North Africa, to command the Free French, plunging de Gaulle into a bitter internecine battle against Giraud, as they became copresidents of the Comité Français de la Libération Nationale.

Churchill very reluctantly supported de Gaulle, who infuriated him but whose escape from France in June 1940 always tipped the balance in his favor, because he admired courage above all other human traits. ("Courage is rightly esteemed the first of human qualities because it is the quality which guarantees the others," Churchill wrote in his book *Great Contemporaries*.)[12] Roosevelt, who believed that de Gaulle had dictatorial tendencies, was particularly infuriated by the way that de Gaulle's actions, such as invading the St. Pierre and Miquelon islands off the coast of Canada on Christmas Day 1941 without warning Washington, threatened the United States' continued diplomatic relations with Vichy France.

Behind his back, Churchill reputedly likened de Gaulle to "a female llama who has been surprised in her bath."[13] There must have been a slightly comic element to the disparity of the two men—who had many titanic rows—arguing face-to-face, since there was a ten-inch disparity between their heights (even without the general's kepi). In November 1944 Cecil Beaton photographed de Gaulle and Churchill inspecting French troops in the Vosges, with snow falling. It is an evocative photograph, but even in his RAF officer's hat, Churchill only came up to de Gaulle's shoulder.

De Gaulle's ingratitude toward his hosts is legendary. "You think I am interested in England winning the war," he told his British liaison officer, General Sir Louis Spears. "I am not. I am only interested in French victory."[14] When Spears simply made the logical remark, "They are the same," de Gaulle replied: "Not at all; not at all in my view." Inspecting French marines at Portsmouth, de Gaulle asked the commanding officer, "Combien des anglais avez-vous ici?" ("How many English do you have here?") The answer came, "Dix-sept, mon general." ("Seventeen, general.") "C'est trop!" replied de Gaulle. ("Too many!")[15] Shortly afterward the commanding officer received an order to reduce the British complement. The story is also told of when de Gaulle visited the devastated city of Stalingrad in 1944, and was asked by a French journalist what he thought. De Gaulle spoke of "a very grand people" and it slowly dawned on the journalist that the general was talking about the Germans, not the Russians, not least when he made the comment: "For them to have come so far."[16]

In June 1943, President Roosevelt wrote to Churchill of de Gaulle, "I am absolutely convinced that he has been and is now injuring our war effort and that he is a very dangerous threat to us. I agree with you that he likes neither the British nor the Americans and that he would doubtless double-cross both of us at the first opportunity."[17] He further thought de Gaulle "a narrow-minded French zealot with too much ambition for his own good and some rather dubious views on democracy."[18] By the time D-Day arrived, the rift between de Gaulle and the Anglo-Saxons was so great that even before any Free French troops had landed in Normandy, he broadcast that this was "France's battle" and entirely failed to mention the other Allies' contribution.

When Churchill briefed him about Operation Overlord on June 4, de Gaulle insisted on various conditions for his support, which began a series of negotiations that became so heated that in the early hours of June 6—as Allied paratroopers were actually dropping over the Normandy beaches—Churchill ordered de Gaulle to be sent back to his headquarters in Algiers "in chains if necessary. He must not be allowed to enter France."[19] It took the British foreign secretary Anthony Eden's best diplomacy to have the order revoked.

De Gaulle admitted to feeling "an anxious pride" in France, and well might he have for a country that was so comprehensively wrecked in the two world wars. Yet because he assumed that France needed greatness in order to *be* France, he simply insisted upon it, whatever the economic and strategic actualities. The British diplomat Lord Gladwyn perceptively pointed out how "undoubtedly the General's chief failing was to cast his country into a role which was beyond her power."[20] But this curious combination of inferiority and superiority complexes not only explains de Gaulle's attitude during the war, but defines the meaning of Gaullism, a political program that is largely bound up in the personality of its founder.

The huge iron Cross of Lorraine at Courseulles-sur-Mer, which is in the middle of Juno beach, where the Canadians landed on D-Day, features a plaque that describes de Gaulle as "the Liberator." The Canadian 3rd Infantry Division commanded by Major General Rodney Keller landed on Juno beach on D-Day against stiff German resistance and waded through beaches soaked with the blood of their comrades to capture all their objectives on the longest day. By contrast, "the Liberator" landed on D+8 and strode ashore to make speeches that barely mentioned the Anglo-Saxon contribution. There is no question who were the true liberators, yet it was essential for French self-respect that a myth should be created, and no one was better at myth creation than Charles de Gaulle.

Consider the statistics: Out of the thirty-nine divisions assigned to the campaign in Normandy, just one was French, the Deuxième Division Blindée (2nd Armored Division) under the command of Major General Jacques-Philippe Leclerc (the nom de guerre of Vicomte Philippe-Marie de Hauteclocque). It fought very bravely to close the Falaise Gap around the Germans in Normandy, but the battle would undoubtedly still have been won without its contribution. The actual military contribution of de Gaulle's forces during the campaign was negligible.

In Führer Directive No. 51 of November 3, 1943, Adolf Hitler concluded, "The danger in the east remains, but a greater danger now appears in the west: an Anglo-Saxon landing."[21] He was correct in the sense that the landings that started the process by which France was freed were primarily made up from the English-speaking peoples. Witness the nationalities of those soldiers killed on D-Day itself: 2,500 Americans, 1,641 Britons, 359 Canadians, 37 Norwegians, 19 Free French, 13 Australians, 2 New Zealanders, and a Belgian. Put another way, of the 4,572 Allied soldiers who gave their lives to liberate France on that momentous day, 0.004 percent were French.

De Gaulle's arrival in France on June 14, more than a week after D-Day, was for only a one-day visit to Bayeux, after which he left for Algiers and did not return to French soil until August 20. In the meantime, General George Patton's Third Army had broken out of Avranches at the end of July and driven through Brittany. The Resistance and Communists—entirely separate organizations from de Gaulle's Free French forces—were doing brave and vital work in support of the Allied forces, especially in hampering German armored retaliation, but de Gaulle played no part in any of this from his base in North Africa.

In a list of his principal worries drawn up just before Operation Overlord began, the Supreme Allied Commander, General

Dwight Eisenhower, placed de Gaulle at the top, even above the uncertainties over the weather in the Channel. For the past four years, de Gaulle had been a perpetual irritant to Allied decision makers, insisting upon being treated as a head of state equal in rank to King George VI and President Roosevelt, even though he was very clearly no such thing. His Free French forces were tiny yet insufferably proud, keen to magnify every minuscule—and often wholly imagined—slight by "les anglo-saxons." In a sense, de Gaulle's sulks were heroic, and patriotic, for in order to protect French self-esteem for the rest of the war and into the postwar years, he had to create the myth of French self-liberation, however untrue and however much it angered Britons and Americans. For political and prestige reasons, de Gaulle begged Eisenhower that French troops be first into Paris; the supreme commander agreed and was as good as his word. Eisenhower did not then visit Paris himself until August 27, partly because he did not wish to detract from de Gaulle's lime-light.

Eisenhower gave the order to Major General Leclerc to advance immediately on Paris on August 22, 1944. He had other units, including the American 4th Division, that could have done it, but he wanted the French to have the glory. De Gaulle meanwhile ordered Leclerc to get to the capital before any Americans arrived. The first of Leclerc's (American-made) Sherman tanks rolled up the rue de Rivoli at 9:30 A.M. on the morning of August 25 and in the surrender document signed that same afternoon between Leclerc and General Dietrich von

Choltitz, the German commander of Paris, there was absolutely no mention made of either Great Britain or the United States.

Once de Gaulle arrived in Paris he made another of the greatest speeches of his life, at the Hôtel de Ville at 5:00 P.M. on the twenty-fifth, in which he cried: "Paris! Outraged Paris! Broken Paris! Martyred Paris! But liberated Paris! Liberated by itself, liberated by its people with the help of the French armies, with the support and the help of all France, of all the France that fights, of the only France, of the real France, of the eternal France!"[22] There was no mention of any Allied contribution until a brief acknowledgment of their existence far into the address, despite the fact that Paris could never have been liberated had it not been for the huge Allied effort in the ten weeks since D-Day. Furthermore, there would never have been an uprising in the capital were Allied troops not within striking distance of it. "Any number of American divisions could more easily have spearheaded our march into Paris," General Omar Bradley recalled afterward. "But to help the French recapture pride, I chose a French force with a tricolor on their Shermans."[23] In his postwar memoirs, Bradley called Paris a pen and ink job on the map.

Major General Leclerc lost a total of seventy-six men killed in the liberation of Paris, although sixteen hundred inhabitants had been killed in the uprising, including six hundred noncombatants. Today the places where the individual soldiers and *résisteurs* fell are marked all over the city. No one would wish to belittle their glorious sacrifice, but the fact remains that the only reason that Leclerc was assigned to the task was because Eisenhower could spare the French 2nd Division from far greater battles that were taking place right across northern and southern France, battles fought against crack German units by British, American, and Canadian forces. They deserved more acknowledgment from de Gaulle.

The next morning—August 26, 1944—Charles de Gaulle led a parade from the Arc de Triomphe down the Champs-Élysées to a thanksgiving service in Notre-Dame Cathedral. When Resistance leaders came abreast of him in the parade he hissed at them to get farther back behind him; the glory was to be his alone. He was cheered to the echo, but of course wartime crowds are fickle; when the collaborationist Vichy president Marshal Philippe Pétain had visited Paris on April 26, 1944— only four months earlier—hundreds of thousands of French people had also turned out to cheer and cry *"Vive le maréchal!"* What France desperately needed was a myth of heroic self-deliverance. That is what de Gaulle gave them in August 1944 and which they came to believe, some of them even to this day. (In August 2004, on the sixtieth anniversary of the liberation of Paris, in a forty-eight-page special commemorative edition of *Le Parisien,* the contribution of the British, Americans, Canadians, and other non-French forces was not even mentioned until page 18, when it was claimed that the Allies had not wanted to liberate Paris at all, but were obliged to send forces there only once the French had effectively liberated themselves.)

As celebrants entered Notre-Dame for that service of thanksgiving for the liberation, shots were fired from inside the cathedral. Everyone dived for cover except de Gaulle, who continued to walk upright at his full height of six foot four toward the altar. It is unclear whether there were Germans still holding out in the cathedral or where else the shots might have come from, but none can doubt the extraordinary physical courage shown by the general on that occasion, as on so many others throughout his life.

"France cannot be France without greatness," General de Gaulle wrote in the opening paragraph of his *War Memoirs*.[24] In 1940–44 there was very little grandeur in France, except in the actions of the French Resistance and of de Gaulle himself and the Free French, who together made up only a small proportion of the population. Nothing can detract from the fact that he had a totally clear view of French national interest, and for him nothing else mattered.

There were some areas in which de Gaulle could never escape the influence of *les anglo-saxons*. When he finally resigned in 1969, he went on holiday to Ireland, where he struck up a friendship with Éamon de Valera, the president of Ireland. They had two things in common: They were both six foot four, and, in the words of the British historian Paul Johnson, "they shared a common hostility and suspicion of England. But there was one difficulty. The only language in which they could converse with any fluency was—English."[25]

When France had to face a fate that thankfully neither Britain nor America, protected by miles of seawater, ever had to,

French people had to come to terms with the Nazi occupation in myriad different ways, comprising everything from total collaboration to full-scale resistance, with the vast penumbra of often-shifting positions in between. The French actress Arletty, when arrested after the liberation for spending the years of the Occupation in the Ritz Hotel with a succession of German officers, explained, *"Mon cœur est français, mais mon cul est international!"* ("My heart is French, but my ass is international!")[26]

If everyone had taken Arletty's stance, France of course could not have survived. Instead, there were men and women who fought on. In many ways de Gaulle was a monster, but he must be regarded as a sacred monster, easily the greatest Frenchman between Napoleon and the present day. It is not given to many people in history to save the honor of their country, but such was the destiny of General de Gaulle. Besides that splendid legacy, all complaints about his ingratitude, hauteur, and pettiness recede. Charles de Gaulle was one of the giants, and we should salute him as such. Despite everything, he was a great man.

CHAPTER EIGHT

DWIGHT D. EISENHOWER

1890–1969

On Saturday, August 8, 1953, Field Marshal Bernard Montgomery visited the British prime ministerial country residence in Buckinghamshire to spend the weekend with his old wartime boss and comrade, Winston Churchill. Over dinner they discussed what one of those present, Churchill's assistant private secretary Jock Colville, termed "the five capital mistakes" that the Americans had made in World War II. It was a favorite topic of conversation for Monty—perhaps *the* favorite—but one that the committed Atlanticist Churchill hardly ever indulged in, partly perhaps because one of America's most important planners of operations during the war, General Dwight D. Eisenhower, had been elected president the previous November.

Montgomery, however, had no such reticence, writing in his memoirs, "I would not class Ike as a great soldier in the true sense of the word. He might have become one if he had ever had the experience of exercising direct command of a division, corps, and army—which unfortunately did not come his way."[1] Monty was fully supported in this uncharitable view by the reliably Yankee-phobic Field Marshal Lord Alan Brooke, who as Sir Alan Brooke had been chief of the imperial general staff from December 1941 until 1946 and who had written in his diary on May 15, 1944, "The main impression I gathered was that Eisenhower was no real director of thought, plans, energy or direction. Just a coordinator, a good mixer, a champion of inter-allied cooperation, and in those respects few can hold the candle to him. But is that enough? Or can we not find all the qualities of a commander in one man?"[2] On the day Brooke wrote that, Eisenhower had briefed King George VI, Churchill, and all the senior chiefs of staff and commanders at St. Paul's School in Hammersmith, London, on the looming Operation Overlord. Not for nothing was Alanbrooke's nickname in the army "Colonel Shrapnel."

The charges against Eisenhower were leveled not only by Britons but also by some distinguished American historians. The double Pulitzer Prize–winning historian Rick Atkinson has recently said of him, "He was not a particularly good field marshal, he was not a Great Captain. Frankly it gnawed at him; he had a lifelong admiration for Hannibal, and he longed to orchestrate a double envelopment, like Cannae. But he lacked the gift of seeing a battlefield in depth spatially and temporally, or of inexorably imposing his operational will on an enemy. There are repeated examples where he simply did not grasp the battle."[3]

It is almost impossible not to like Ike, with his cheery countenance, relentlessly can-do optimism, and his insistence on absolute equality between Americans and Britons on his staff. His naval aide, Captain Harry C. Butcher, recalled him reprimanding an American officer for quarreling with his British counterpart: "I forgive you for calling him a son-of-a-bitch. But I cannot forgive you for calling him a *British* son-of-a-bitch."[4] On the occasion at St. Paul's School cited earlier, Eisenhower had closed his remarks with the joke "In half an hour Hitler will have missed his one and only chance of destroying with a single well-aimed bomb the entire high command of the Allied forces."[5] Yet however much one likes Ike, one must address the criticisms of him made by his British counterparts and by modern American historians such as Atkinson.

WHAT WERE THE SUPPOSED "five capital mistakes" made by the United States in the western theater of World War II that Churchill and Monty enunciated together that summer evening in 1953? To quote Colville:

1. They had prevented [General Sir Harold] Alexander getting to Tunis the first time, when he could easily have done so.

2. They had done at Anzio what [General Sir Frederick] Stopford did at Suvla Bay [on the Gallipoli Peninsula in 1915]: clung to the beaches and failed to establish positions inland as they could well have done. Churchill said he wanted it to be a mainly-British operation.

3. They had insisted on Operation Anvil [the attack on the French Riviera in August 1944], thereby preventing Alexander from taking Trieste and Vienna.

4. Eisenhower had refused to let Monty, in Overlord, concentrate his advance on the left flank. He had insisted on a broad advance, which could not be supported, and had thus allowed Rundstedt to counter-attack on the Ardennes and had prolonged the war, with dire political results, to the spring of 1945.

5. Eisenhower had let the Russians occupy Berlin, Prague and Vienna—all of which might have been entered by the Americans.[6]

Yet when one examines this seemingly formidable indictment sheet, much of its apparent power slips away:

1. It was Monty himself who let the Afrika Korps escape after El Alamein; his slow pursuit allowed the Germans time to defend Tunis. Although Alexander's was a different operation, Montgomery sounds like he was covering himself for something for which he was more guilty than the Americans.

2. The Stopford analogy at Anzio was a good one and very Churchillian, relating as it does to the disaster at Suvla Bay that clearly still rankled him nearly forty years later. But the American general at Anzio, John P. Lucas, was sacked by General Mark Clark, and Churchill was wrong to claim that it could ever have been a British operation, as the U.S. Fifth Army was on the west coast of Italy and the British Eighth Army on the east, and the Americans had the shipping and available men.

3. True, Anvil was an unnecessary diversion, but Alexander did eventually take Trieste. Whether he could have repeated Napoleon's 1797 campaign and marched on Vienna (which Napoleon never actually reached on that campaign) is highly debatable, and in any case the Russians gave up Vienna on the day they promised to. Marshall could be criticized in his selection of Mark Clark, whose obsession with taking Rome before D-Day allowed the Germans to escape capture after the success of Operation Diadem, but not for opposing the Balkans plan, which only promised much more of the same kind of fighting, especially around the so-called Ljubljana Gap.

4. The main criticism of Eisenhower in late 1944 and 1945 is that the broad front strategy that Eisenhower adopted for the invasion of Germany lengthened the war because it left the Allies with too few places that military strategists call the *Schwerpunkt* or *point d'appui*,

the single place of decisive main effort. It meant that scarce supplies were spread out thinly instead of being massed at a point ripe for a breakthrough. The accusation some make is that being unable or unwilling to choose among Montgomery, Patton, and Bradley over who should lead a narrow thrust, he chose none of them. Yet this, too, is unfair: Operation Market Garden was precisely such a thrust, and it failed comprehensively. The only time Eisenhower gave in to Monty on the broad front versus narrow thrust had, therefore, ended in fiasco, so it was understandable why he was unwilling to try it again, or to let Patton do the same in the south. He also needed to avoid another Ardennes by keeping up pressure all along the line and not allowing in February or March 1945 any recurrence of what had happened in December 1944 and January 1945. After the hard-won but undeniable victory in the Battle of the Bulge, there was still hard fighting in February 1945 between the River Ruhr and the Rhine. Very bad weather grounded aircraft and flooded the fields, and intelligence about the nature of likely German resistance inside Germany itself was patchy. "Eisenhower is to blame for the broad-front strategy that stretched Allied lines so thin that German armor had little difficulty breaking through," writes an American biographer of his, Jean Edward Smith, in an otherwise admiring biography, claiming that Eisenhower should not have let the Germans get as far as they did before counterattacking.[7] In fact, the Ardennes offensive was a thirty-nine-divisional surprise attack carried out under complete radio silence, through three feet of snow, with searchlights bounced off the 100 percent cloud cover to turn night into day and prevent Allied air superiority from being brought to bear. Nothing could have prevented the Wehrmacht from getting to the Meuse; indeed, it took astonishing courage in places like Bastogne to slow their advance and to prevent their reaching the English Channel. Had Eisenhower adopted the alternative strategy of deep thin thrusts across the Rhine, the Allies would have been stretched even tighter.

5. It was simply not true to say that Eisenhower "let" the Russians occupy Berlin, Prague, and Vienna, because each had already been earmarked for the Russians by joint Allied-Russian commissions starting even before Yalta. The Russians suffered more than eighty thousand casualties taking Berlin, numbers that the Western Allies preferred not to suffer, and it is a myth to suppose that the Germans were going to lay down their arms before the Americans had they got there earlier. "Personally and aside from all logistical, tactical, or strategical implications," Marshall wrote to Eisenhower in April 1945, "I would be loath to hazard American lives for purely political purposes."[8] As Churchill's

deputy military secretary Sir Ian Jacob put it, "His [Marshall's] idea was to bring the war to an end as quickly as possible, bring the boys home and let the politicians pick up the pieces." It was an understandable reaction.

General George Patton could be cutting about Eisenhower, jealously joking that the "D.D." in Ike's name must stand for "Divine Destiny" because his constant promotions happened without his having commanded any troops in the field. Yet Eisenhower was denied the chance of active service in World War I and had to command the American landings in North Africa in 1942 from a cave in Gibraltar, so it is perfectly true that the first time he saw a shot fired in anger was when he shot a rat in his headquarters at Caserta in Italy in 1943. But most of the troops in Operation Torch had not seen action, either, and much of his insistence on good discipline stemmed from that knowledge. As Supreme Allied Commander in Europe, Eisenhower had overall control of 4.5 million American and 1 million other Allied troops in 91 divisions, 28,000 aircraft, 970,000 vehicles, and 18 million tons of supplies. At that level of command, war fighting was about much more than having been in combat in one's youth. Above all, it required huge delegation at the substrategic and the tactical levels, which simply in terms of natural justice means that the supreme commander cannot be blamed for every reverse.

When considering Patton's malicious comments about his

commander, one must factor in Eisenhower's statement about Patton's famous face-slapping incident, that "it raised serious doubts about his future usefulness as a commander."[9] Yet Eisenhower had not sacked Patton, recognizing that generals of his quality were in short supply.

Harder to defend Eisenhower against are the criticisms by Atkinson, of the moments

> when the Germans and Italians escaped from Sicily across the Straits of Messina in August 1943; when [Eisenhower] approved a hare-brained scheme to drop the 82nd Airborne Division on Rome in September 1943 with the nearest substantial supporting ground force landing at Salerno two hundred miles away; when . . . various missteps by the high command led to part of the German force escaping from the so-called Falaise Gap in Normandy in August 1944; and when he failed to heed clear warnings about the importance of capturing the estuarial approaches to Antwerp—the River Scheldt—in addition to the city itself, so that when Allied forces captured this absolutely vital port intact in early September 1944, the Germans kept the approaches and the port was useless for almost three more months.[10]

Like Monty's, this looks like a formidable rap sheet, yet German escapes from such tight corners as the Messina Straits and the Falaise Gap were an indication more of the continued strong discipline and professionalism of the Wehrmacht in retreat than any failure of Eisenhower's strategic sense, just as the German capacity for counterattack constantly had to be guarded against. The 82nd Airborne wasn't in the end dropped on Rome, when last-minute intelligence made it appear that the negotiations then being held between General Maxwell Taylor and Marshal Pietro Badoglio might be an Axis trap. (They weren't.)

Instead, the 82nd Airborne Division was kept back for Operation Overlord. A month before D-Day, the air commander in chief, British Air Marshal Sir Trafford Leigh-Mallory, warned Eisenhower that the 82nd was courting disaster on the projected sites for gliders on dangerous landing areas against tough German opposition miles behind enemy lines on the Cotentin Peninsula. Although Eisenhower didn't disagree with Leigh-Mallory's projections, he would not change the plan, and replied by saying, "A strong airborne attack in the region indicated is essential to the success of the whole operation and it must go on."[11] It was, and it did, and it seriously disrupted the German attempt to reinforce the peninsula, at a high but not unacceptable cost.

The tardiness in freeing up the vital supply route along the Scheldt to Antwerp can indeed be laid at Eisenhower's door. The amount of fuel that was consumed bringing ammunition, weapons, troops, supplies, and equipment to the battlefields of northwestern France, and thus subsequently Germany, all the way from the Mulberry Harbors would have been cut in half had it all been able to come straight across the Channel and down the Scheldt. Yet to set against that was the stout German resistance in the area; they knew the strategic importance of Antwerp as well as he did, and the Scheldt is fifty miles long from its mouth to Antwerp.

In Eisenhower's defense, what he was trying to do had never been attempted before in history. The integration of the Allied command structure alone was unprecedented. In the First World War, planning and execution had been left up to individual armies in individual sectors, so this was a revolutionary way for a campaign to be fought. As Churchill put it in his war memoirs: "At no time has the principle of alliance between noble races been carried and maintained at so high a pitch."[12] The advice Eisenhower gave Admiral Lord Louis Mountbatten when he took over as Supreme Allied Commander of the South East Asia Command perfectly illustrates his challenge. "Never permit any problem to be approached in your staff on the basis of national interest," Eisenhower ordered.

> An Allied Commander-in-Chief must be self-effacing, quick to give credit, ready to meet the other fellow more than half way and absorb advice and must be willing to decentralize. . . . He is in a very definite sense the Chairman of the Board, a Chairman that has very definite executive responsibilities. The point I make is that while the set-up may be somewhat artificial, and not

always so clean-cut as you might desire, your personality and good sense must make it work.[13]

Eisenhower was a good picker of men and was enormously helped in this by one of his best personnel choices, Walter Bedell Smith, one of the great chiefs of staff in American history. Although Eisenhower was good at delegating, a vital prerequisite in such a job, he was careful never to cede ultimate control. One of his few resignation threats came two months before D-Day over a British attempt to redirect the activities of the bomber force that was softening up targets in Normandy and the Pas de Calais. He made a few resignation threats to his diary—which do not count—such as when he wrote: "I am tired of dealing with a lot of prima donnas. By God, you tell that bunch that if they can't get together and stop quarrelling like children, I will tell the Prime Minister to get someone else to run this damn war."[14]

George Patton once said, "God deliver us from our friends. We can handle the enemy," and the senior Allied commanders were indeed prima donnas, Patton himself vying with Monty as the worst of all.[15] Bradley had "total disdain" for Monty and contempt for Patton, who in turn was "sickened" when Monty became a field marshal. Monty meanwhile despised both Patton and Bradley. Despite constant and extreme provocations, Eisenhower somehow held the ring successfully until V-E Day. Furthermore, in an army where George Patton, Omar Bradley, Mark Clark, Albert Wedemeyer, and Orlando Ward thoroughly detested the British, Ike actually liked them. One can quite understand why Britons like Monty and Brooke might not be everyone's cup of tea—or "tiffin" as Eisenhower called it, and by the time he left England he had also learned "petrol" rather than "gasoline"—but it was necessary that the person at the top did get on with his hosts. It irritated Americans hugely; Patton even sneered that "Ike's the best damn general the British have got."[16]

Criticism from the British press that he was too cautious a commander did not alarm Eisenhower, but left him tired and mildly irritated. "It wearies me to be thought of as timid, when I've had to do things that were so risky as to be almost crazy," he wrote on February 7, 1944, probably thinking of the attacks on Salerno and Pantelleria.[17] Early in 1944 he complained in his diary, "They dislike to believe that I had anything particularly to do with the campaigns. They don't use the words 'initiative' and 'boldness' in talking of me, but often do in speaking of Monty."[18] And then he merely wrote, "Oh hum."

The hide of a pachyderm is necessary to a great commander, and Eisenhower certainly had one. He was outwardly calm in every crisis, something that he learned from his period in the Philippines in the late 1930s, which he described as "learning dramatics under Douglas MacArthur." For all that Eisenhower came to dislike MacArthur personally while serving under him, he nonetheless learned how to conduct himself as a great man, and how not to, in Churchill's phrase, "fall below the level of events."

Yet the secret of Eisenhower's success can be summed up in two words—"George Marshall"—whose protégé he was. Having been a major for sixteen years when Marshall discovered him, Eisenhower then ascended from lieutenant colonel to five-star general in only forty-two months, an average of six months between promotions. The regular officers in the prewar army did see rapid promotion: In 1939 there were only fifteen thousand officers in the U.S. Army; by 1944 there were thirteen hundred generals. But it was not all easy for Eisenhower. In January 1943, a month before the defeat at Kasserine Pass, the relative lack of success in North Africa after the initially successful Operation Torch landing led his aide, Harry Butcher, to write, "His neck is in a noose and he knows it." Patton wrote in his diary that Eisenhower "thinks his thread is about to be cut." Soon afterward, Eisenhower wrote to his son John, "It will not break my heart and it should not cause you any mental anguish. . . . Modern war is a very complicated business and governments are forced to treat individuals as pawns."[19] Yet throughout these moments, George Marshall stood by Eisenhower and believed in him.

For all Marshall's support, Eisenhower knew he was expendable if he did not perform well. After sacking his friend General Lloyd Fredendall of II Corps when Rommel had defeated him in Tunisia, Eisenhower wrote to his replacement, George Patton, "This matter frequently calls for more courage than any other thing you will have to do, but I expect you to be perfectly cold-blooded about it."[20] If he couldn't always sack a general, he could sometimes damn him with faint praise: When in early 1945 Marshall asked Eisenhower to place in order of value all the senior generals in the European theater of operations, he ranked Lieutenant General Jacob L. Devers, the commander of the 6th Army Group, twenty-fourth on the list.

Eisenhower had a good deal of common sense and much emotional intelligence, something that was not the case with a surprisingly large number of senior commanders. Montgomery belittled the American contribution to the Battle of the Bulge at a press conference; Patton slapped two soldiers suffering from shell shock and was generally unhinged by the end of the war; MacArthur had no concept of how others saw him; Mountbatten tried to sack General William Slim, the best and most beloved general in the British Army. Eisenhower, meanwhile, showed perfectly mature judgment throughout campaign after exhausting campaign. "It is impossible to read his correspondence," notes the historian Correlli Barnett, "without being impressed with the good sense, energy and all-round capability which he applied to problems ranging widely from high allied policy to inter-allied relations; to military discipline, training and tactics; and to logistics, especially the available lift by road and air."[21]

Eisenhower was a decision maker. It was he who signed off on all the major planning decisions for Operation Overlord, which was easily the largest and most complicated multinational, triservice amphibious landing in the history of warfare. Yet despite the pressure of having tens of thousands of lives hanging on his decisions, he kept calm. "A sense of humor and a great faith, or else a complete lack of imagination," he joked, "are essential to sanity."[22] He had enough imagination to think the unthinkable and to write out a communiqué that would state that in the event of D-Day's turning out badly, "The troops, the air and the navy did all that bravery and devotion to duty can do. If blame attaches to the attempt, it is mine alone." Douglas MacArthur, in his evaluation of Eisenhower in 1932, wrote that he was "distinguished by force, judgment and willingness to accept responsibility," and never more so was that true than in the draft communiqué, which he left in his pocket and forgot about.

After the original attack date of June 5 for D-Day had to be postponed the very day before, on June 4, Eisenhower had to take the decision on June 5 as to whether to launch the invasion on the sixth, on the basis of the projections of a British meteorologist, Group Captain James Stagg, who told him that June 6 would see fine weather, which would then worsen after that vital day. The window was small, and Stagg's conclusion was not unanimously supported by the whole meteorological team. "This is a decision I alone can take," Eisenhower told his staff. "After all, that is what I am here for. We will sail tomorrow."[23] He was smoking four packets of cigarettes a day at the time, and in July had a blood pressure of 176 over 110—indicating high-risk, stage two hypertension. Yet such were his leadership skills that none of his troops seem to have noticed it.

After the battles of Caen and the Falaise Gap came the great debate between the broad front versus the narrow thrust strategy for the next stage of the campaign, the advance into Germany. Put crudely, Montgomery wanted to use the logistic reserves and part of Bradley's 12th Army Group to join his own 21st Army Group to send a forty-divisional force north of the Ardennes to capture the Ruhr in a narrow but fast thrust that would deprive Germany of much of its manufacturing base. Yet there were three great rivers in Holland—the Rhine, the Maas, and the Waal—that had not been crossed, and the whole of the rest of the front would need to halt if Monty was to get his way. Furthermore, by the end of September continued German resistance along the Atlantic Wall meant that only the ports of Cherbourg and Antwerp were in Allied hands. The latter was unusable because of the continued German presence on the Scheldt, and only one Mulberry Harbor was operational after a storm had damaged the other one soon after D-Day.

Any narrow thrust, therefore, would be in danger of being attacked from flanking counterstrokes, or even of being completely cut off and surrounded; the Germans would show in the Ardennes in December 1944 that they still had plenty of fight left in them. Eisenhower even suspected, as he told Marshall, that Montgomery was only making the proposal "based on wishful thinking" and to commandeer the maximum amount of resources possible. Another factor—the fear of Patton's trying to make the same maneuver farther south—might also have motivated Montgomery. Nonetheless, despite Eisenhower's clear-sighted view of Montgomery's motives, he did authorize Montgomery's disastrous Market Garden Operation that destroyed the British 1st Airborne Division at Arnhem in late September, in a smaller version of what might well have happened to Montgomery's narrow thrust into the Ruhr.

At No. 10 Downing Street in late 1944, at a conference with Churchill and the British chiefs, including Brooke, Eisenhower explained the logic behind his broad front strategy, in contrast to the one advocated by Montgomery. Brooke used the same phrase then that he had used two years earlier at the Casablanca Conference—"I flatly disagree"—but now Eisenhower marshaled all his facts and outargued Brooke, to the satisfaction of everyone except Brooke (and his always readable but often poisonous diary).

The broad front strategy approach was finally vindicated in late March 1945, by which time all German resistance west of the Rhine had been pulverized into submission. Back on March 8, Eisenhower confirmed that the 21st Army Group should cross the Rhine at Wesel on March 24, and that Jacob Devers's 6th Army Group should initiate operations in the Saar, which would establish bridgeheads over the Rhine in the Mainz-Mannheim sector. This involved the U.S. general Alexander Patch breaking through the Siegfried Line and taking part in a massive pincer movement, with Patton's Third Army attacking toward the Rhine near Koblenz, which managed to surround the German Seventh Army and take 107,000 prisoners. Eisenhower's strategy resulted in the capture of 280,000 German prisoners. With Bradley's 12th Army Group thrusting toward Frankfurt

and German industry effectively no longer producing arma-
ments for the Reich, it was only a matter of time before Germany surrendered.

At the end of March the last great Anglo-American strategic
argument took place, when Eisenhower wanted to agree with
Stalin on a line from Erfurt through Leipzig to Dresden for the
junction of the Anglo-American forces with the Red Army.
Churchill and Montgomery wanted to take advantage of the
German collapse in the west to cross the Elbe and advance as far
eastward as possible, even possibly taking Berlin before the Russians. Churchill wanted this for political reasons; the Russians
were about to take Vienna, and if they took Berlin, too, he argued to Roosevelt on April 1, it would "lead them into a mood
which will raise grave and formidable difficulties in the future."[24]

At that point, Red Army forces were 45 miles from Berlin
while Eisenhower's were 250 miles. A race to Berlin would have
been extraordinarily costly and, unless the Western powers
were willing to face down the Red Army and rip up the already
agreed demarcation agreements—which was politically unthinkable at that time—ultimately worthless.

Eisenhower did not get everything right, by any means.
When he left the Mediterranean theater to command the invasion of France, he told reporters that Hitler was "going to write
off this southern front, and I don't think he is going to defend it
long."[25] Of course generals needed to be upbeat when speaking
to journalists, but much more tellingly he told his diary on September 5, 1944, "The defeat of the German armies is complete,"

over eight very bloody months before it genuinely was.[26] Yet overall, he got more important things right than anyone else, which is what the Allies needed in a supreme commander.

Roosevelt chose Eisenhower as supreme commander in January 1944 because he was both a natural leader and also someone with exceptional political instincts. Generals need also to be statesmen and in wartime politicians have to be strategists, because there is no clear divide between politics and strategy in modern war any more than there was in ancient times, when the post of *strategos*, or general, in fifth-century B.C. Athens implied political leadership as well as naval or military. Eisenhower was ideal in both roles, as his successful presidency also shows. As we have seen with Napoleon, Churchill, and others, the qualities needed in a successful soldier are often complementary to those for a successful politician, and they, too, coalesced in Dwight Eisenhower.

In the spring of 1944 Eisenhower wrote to his wife, Mamie—they were the only letters he didn't dictate—wondering, "How many youngsters are gone forever. A man must develop a veneer of callousness that lets him consider such things dispassionately."[27] But it was only ever a veneer. Eisenhower was a fundamentally decent man. In 1926, fifteen years before World War II, he had graduated from the Command and General Staff College at Fort Leavenworth, Kansas, top out of 245 candidates, an achievement that would have given anyone a sense of superiority—though Eisenhower never let his show. He experienced several setbacks in his life, often thinking that he was serving in backwaters, but he never allowed these to embitter him. Considering that he did not see action in either world war, his achievement in ending up as the senior serving Allied officer was truly remarkable.

Engraved over his tomb in Abilene, Kansas—which is only twenty miles from the geographical center of the United States—are the words he spoke at London's Guildhall a month after V-E Day: "Humility must always be the portion of any man who receives acclaim earned in blood of his followers and sacrifices of his friends." They are noble words and ones that no soldier or statesman should forget.

After General Alfred Jodl signed the unconditional surrender at Eisenhower's headquarters at Reims, Ike wrote with admirable humility, accuracy, and some terseness to the Combined Chiefs of Staff to report: "The mission of this Allied force was fulfilled at 02.41 local time, May 7th 1945." Marshall replied, "You have commanded with outstanding success the most powerful military force that has ever been assembled. You have made history, great history for the good of all Mankind, and you have stood for all we hope for and admire in an officer of the United States Army."[28] Notwithstanding the occasionally justified criticisms of some modern historians, and to a far lesser extent the sniping of his contemporaries and rivals, there is not one word of Marshall's estimation that needs to be altered today, more than seventy years after it was written. It deserves to be the settled historical verdict on Dwight D. Eisenhower.

———

CHAPTER NINE

MARGARET THATCHER

1925–2013

Margaret Thatcher's ultimate hero was Churchill—just as one of Churchill's was Napoleon. She was fourteen years old in that *annus mirabilis* of 1940 when she sat beside the radio in the upper room above her father's grocery store listening to Churchill's speeches during the Blitz and the Battle of Britain. Those years up to early teenage are very important in the political makeup of a statesman, indeed far more so than the late-teenage years that biographers tend to concentrate upon much more. For it is then when international events first impinge on the young consciousness, and lessons are consciously or subconsciously learned. Napoleon was fourteen when the American War of Independence was won against Britain, Churchill was twelve when Queen Victoria celebrated her Golden Jubilee, and

Charles de Gaulle's earliest political memories were of his father's raging against the British over the Fashoda crisis on the Upper Nile.

Similarly, Margaret Thatcher was twelve years old when her parents, Alfred and Beatrice Roberts, took a young German Jewish girl into their home in 1938, just before Kristallnacht, so young Margaret was never under any illusions about the true nature of fascism. Alderman Roberts was a Methodist lay preacher who believed it was his community's duty to give practical help to the persecuted of other lands regardless of race or religion, and by taking in that young Jewish refugee from the Nazis he almost certainly saved her life. She herself certainly thought so and was profoundly grateful to the Thatcher family for the rest of her days. It taught Margaret about the superiority of decisive practical action over mere hand-wringing and vapid moralizing, of the kind that all too many appeasers—in the 1930s and since—have been guilty. Critics and cynics who claim that Margaret's philo-Semitism stemmed from political motives—as a member of Parliament she sat for the largely Jewish constituency of Finchley North—ignore this crucially formative influence on her.

Margaret Thatcher was only twenty-four in February 1950 when she doughtily fought the Dartford constituency in Kent for the Conservative Party, gaining much national media attention in the process. "She campaigned with energy and determination," records a biographer, and cut the Labour majority from 19,714 to 13,638. Although she was not to enter the House of

Commons until 1959, her path was set. It was not until the early 1970s, however, that she found her true cause in the free market economics and pugnacious patriotism that were to characterize her more than eleven years in the premiership after May 1979.

When in April 1982 the fascist junta that ruled Argentina—several members of which had been responsible for the disappearance and murder of tens of thousands of Argentinians in the 1970s—suddenly and without any warning invaded the Falkland Islands in the South Atlantic, they failed to take into account the mettle of their opponent. No prime minister had taken Britain to war since Anthony Eden's disastrous adventure at Suez over a quarter of a century before.

Whereas every British prime minister since Churchill would probably have tried to do a deal with the Argentinians, Margaret Thatcher had the courage to see the conflict in stark black-and-white terms, as a matter of duty and national honor about which no compromise was possible. (When the previous December the Foreign Office had suggested that she congratulate the Argentine junta on taking office, she replied that British premiers do not send messages "on the occasion of military takeovers.")[1] She was entirely unaffected by what has been termed "the policy of the pre-emptive cringe," which had been the default position of successive British governments ever since the Suez humiliation.

Not everyone saw the Falklands in the stark, almost Manichean terms that Thatcher did. There were only eighteen hundred inhabitants of the islands, who led a hardscrabble, mainly agricultural existence in the rain-swept South Atlantic. Indeed, the great Argentine writer Jorge Luis Borges famously likened the struggle to "two bald men fighting over a comb."[2] That would be fair were it not for the fact that there was also a matter of profound principle at stake: British territory had been invaded and the liberty of Britons violated. If Britain was to retain her honor and prestige in the world, this could not be allowed to stand.

For the Falklands had been a British colony since 1765; many families living there could trace their British ancestry back almost nine generations. The United Nations had stated in 1960 that the islanders' self-determination was paramount, and their wishes had been made evident in several referenda in which 99.8 percent of them voted to remain British.

Yet there are still some people today who believe that the Falklands should belong to Argentina, regardless of the wishes of their inhabitants. In 2012 the actor Sean Penn wrote an article in the *Guardian* demanding that the United Kingdom renounce her sovereignty over the Falklands.[3] Many *Guardian* readers probably supported what Penn was suggesting, and back in 1982 there were others in the decision-making bodies of the British state who were similarly willing to ignore the unanimous and oft-repeated desire of the islanders to remain British. "In the eyes of the Foreign and Commonwealth Office," notes one study of the conflict, by Max Hastings and Simon Jenkins, "they could not possibly weigh heavily against British policy towards South America, a continent of 240 millions."[4] Because the islands were more than 8,000 miles from Britain but only 400 miles from Argentina—which called them Las Malvinas—the British Foreign Office was prepared to consider ceding sovereignty over them with a form of lease-back agreement, in order for Britain to stay popular with Latin America. But they had not reckoned with a prime minister among whose sayings was "If you just set out to be liked, you would be prepared to compromise on anything, wouldn't you, at any time? And you would achieve nothing!"[5]

In one sense, Margaret Thatcher was herself partly responsible for the decision of General Leopoldo Galtieri, the head of the junta, to invade the Falklands. Defense cuts had led the Ministry of Defence to withdraw the ice-patrol vessel HMS *Endurance*, which had been purchased from Denmark in 1967, at the end of its 1981–82 tour, producing a saving of more than $2.5 million a year. Margaret Thatcher had supported the Ministry of Defence over this. It is believed that the Argentine junta saw the withdrawal of *Endurance* as an indication that the British were in the process of climbing down from their international commitments to their colonies. The cost of the Falklands War eventually came to more than $7 billion: Rarely has the truth been more starkly displayed that relatively high defense spending represents good value for money, because combat is always far more expensive than deterrence.

The junta's decision to invade the islands on Friday, April 2, 1982, was not finally made until Wednesday, March 31, only two days earlier, but the Secret Intelligence Service (SIS, also known as MI6) did manage to warn Thatcher and the foreign secretary, Lord Carrington, on Sunday, March 28, that Argentine naval and equipment movements, and naval and diplomatic Easter leave cancellations, implied that they might. As they left for a European Union meeting in Brussels, Thatcher and Carrington discussed SIS's warning, from which the Joint Intelligence Committee had nonetheless concluded that no invasion was imminent. Together, they agreed to send three nuclear submarines south, including HMS *Conqueror.* Even though the submarines sailed at the impressive average speed of 23 knots, the first one still could not take up station off the Falklands capital, Stanley, until April 12, and so were unable to affect events in the short term.

On March 31 signals intelligence showed SIS that an Argentine fleet had put to sea and an attack must be expected within forty-eight hours. In a four-hour meeting in Mrs. Thatcher's room in the House of Commons at 7:00 that night—with Permanent Under-Secretary at the Ministry of Defence Sir Frank Cooper being summoned from a dinner party to attend—they reviewed the reports and the Joint Intelligence Committee's view that invasion was still by no means a certainty. The British ambassador to Washington, Sir Nicolas Henderson, took the intelligence reports to President Reagan's secretary of state, Alexander Haig, who asked his CIA liaison officer, "Why have I not been told of this?" At 9:00 P.M., Mrs. Thatcher telegraphed President Reagan to ask him to warn Galtieri off British sovereign territory, but Galtieri refused to take Reagan's call.

Most of the seven men in the PM's room at the House of Commons counseled caution. One hesitates to generalize about matters to do with gender, but for an historian it is hard not to sympathize at least in part with the thrust of Rudyard Kipling's poem about how "the female of the species is deadlier than the male"—as it happens, one of Margaret Thatcher's favorite poems. Boudica, Elizabeth I, Catherine de Medici, Catherine the Great, Maria Theresa, Golda Meir, Indira Gandhi, Margaret Thatcher: The witness of history is virtually uniform in the willingness of female decision makers to fight, once they have decided the cause is just and/or necessary.

At the meeting in the prime minister's room, the Foreign Office representatives said that Mrs. Thatcher should give the Argentinians no excuses by being provocative. Secretary of State for Defence Sir John Nott pointed out all the logistical difficulties of carrying out an operation eight thousand miles away from the home base. Once sent, it was pointed out, any task force would be politically very hard to recall. It would involve putting almost all of Britain's naval forces in one basket, would cost Britain a fortune (during a bad recession), would be unpopular internationally, could strain relations with the United States (whose ambassador to the UN, Jeane Kirkpatrick, was known to favor the Argentinians), and there was of course always the danger of suffering defeat at the hands of Argentina's large surface fleet, four submarines, armed forces entrenched on the islands, and their two hundred modern warplanes flown by brave and resourceful pilots.

At that crucial meeting, only Mrs. Thatcher was instinctively averse to the cautious approach. But then reinforcements arrived in the sharp, spare, no-nonsense form of Admiral of the Fleet Sir Henry Leach, the First Sea Lord and chief of the navy staff, who has been described as "very much an admiral's admiral."[6] The Royal Navy has a long tradition of straight-talking admirals. One might instance the earl of St. Vincent, who famously said during the Napoleonic Wars: "I do not say the French cannot come, I only say *they cannot come by sea*."[7] Or Admiral Lord Cunningham during World War II, who, when told that it would be very costly to evacuate the British Army from Crete, replied: "It takes the Navy three years to build a ship. It will take three hundred years to build a new tradition. The evacuation will continue."[8]

Admiral Leach had arrived by helicopter from Portsmouth, where he had been carrying out an official engagement and was, therefore, wearing the full-dress admiral's uniform, giving him further authority in a room full of civilians. His arrival completely changed the tenor of the meeting, greatly to Thatcher's benefit. She asked him if he could mobilize a task force to liberate the Falklands if they were invaded. Leach said he could, and by the weekend—the meeting was taking place on a Wednesday night—and he added that the navy not only could but should respond to an invasion. When Thatcher asked him what he would do if he was the Argentine admiral, Leach replied, "I would return to harbour immediately."[9] Thatcher seized on this with her characteristic forcefulness whenever she saw a political opening. The Royal Navy fleet was put on immediate alert. A senior Ministry of Defence official later joked, "Every one of Leach's commanders would have been shot if those ships had not been ready to sail by the weekend. Leach knew that not just the Falklands were at stake." For what else was at stake was the Royal Navy's reputation, the survival of the Thatcher ministry, and, at a much deeper level, the country's honor. This was something that was instinctively grasped by Margaret Thatcher, who, without approval from either Parliament or even her own cabinet, that night ordered Leach, "The task force is to be made ready."[10] It did indeed set sail that Sunday, April 4. In the meantime, President Reagan spoke to Galtieri for an hour, impressing on him Mrs. Thatcher's resolve to resist any invasion. He offered his vice president, George Bush, as a mediator, but was refused.

There had been almost no Royal Navy contingency planning for a campaign such as one to recapture the Falklands, which had featured very low on the list of likely Cold War conflicts. This was possibly why no ultimatum was given to Argentina, or indeed any direct message made by Britain before the invasion itself. At dawn on Friday, April 2, the Argentinians landed and imprisoned the populations of the capital, Stanley, and other places. The day before, the island's governor, Rex Hunt, had summoned two British officers—the two majors in charge of eighty marines—and told them, "It looks as if the buggers mean it."[11] The marines were overwhelmed by forces one hundred times their number, and, although some shots were fired, they were ordered by Hunt to surrender. This was felt to be a humiliation back in Britain, but there was no practical military alternative, as the geography of the islands provided no cover for guerrilla action.

The British cabinet immediately went into emergency, indeed almost continual, session. Mrs. Thatcher now required total support from a cabinet that over many other issues over the past three years had all too often withheld it from her. So in order to identify and hopefully neutralize dissent, she went around the cabinet table asking for the views of each minister in turn, rather than allowing the more forceful of them to proffer a collective view. They said that the naval task force should not be sent if it was only going to be turned around again in mid-ocean. No cabinet minister thought that the outcome would be war: Everyone assumed either that the crisis would be dealt with diplomatically via Washington or that the Argentinians would back down unilaterally. As Deputy Prime Minister Willie Whitelaw said, if the fleet was stood down once it had sailed but without a deal, the government would have to resign over the national humiliation. Thatcher got the support of her cabinet on the basis that once it had sailed, the task force would expel the Argentinians from the Falklands either by force or by the threat of it.

The House of Commons had not sat on a Saturday since the Suez crisis, but it was recalled for Saturday, April 3, when Mrs. Thatcher announced, "A large Task Force will sail as soon as preparations are complete," and that her government's object was "to see the Islands returned to British administration."[12] During that debate, Ulster Unionist MP Enoch Powell referred to the sobriquet "Iron Lady" that the Russians had bestowed on her, and said that in the coming weeks Thatcher herself, the House of Commons, and the rest of the world "would learn of what mettle she is made."

On Monday, April 5, Carrington and two other Foreign and Commonwealth ministers, Humphrey Atkins and Richard Luce, resigned under the principle of collective responsibility, even though Atkins and Luce had not been responsible for the policy toward Argentina or the withdrawal of *Endurance*. Thatcher appointed the liberal Tory MP Francis Pym in Carrington's place, and almost instantly regretted it. She also set up a small war cabinet consisting of herself, Whitelaw, Pym, John Nott, and Cecil Parkinson, the chairman of the Conservative Party. Parkinson gave her a 3–2 majority against the liberal Tories— then known as the Wets in British public school speak—in case things turned difficult. Whitelaw, the leading Wet, recalled shuddering every time he thought of Suez during the Falklands crisis.

In the UN Security Council, Britain was in a difficult position. Sir Anthony Parsons, the British ambassador, moved Resolution 502, demanding the "immediate withdrawal" of Argentine forces, but although he could count on the support of the United States, France, Ireland, and Japan, he knew that the Communist bloc of China, Russia, and Poland could be relied upon to vote against. The Latin countries Spain and Panama openly supported Argentina. That meant Parsons had to win over all five of the other members—Jordan, Togo, Zaire, Uganda, and Guyana—in order to win the two-thirds majority necessary for the resolution to pass, and he had only forty-eight hours in which to do it.

Parsons managed it. France had to put pressure on Togo and Mrs. Thatcher needed to telephone King Hussein of Jordan directly. He put the betting at 6 to 4 against that the Russians would use their Security Council veto, but despite severe Argentine pressure over grain sales, they did not, because ideologically they did not want to be seen siding with an authoritarian right-wing regime against a democracy. Mrs. Thatcher, though no fan of the United Nations, could henceforward state that "all the Argentinians need to do is honour UN Security Council 502." This she did very regularly throughout the coming fraught days and weeks.

General Haig did his very best on behalf of peace with shuttle diplomacy between the soon-to-be combatants, but found that the Argentinians would not permit any element of self-determination for the Falkland Islanders in the future and refused to allow the Argentine flag to be hauled down there under any circumstances. In his meetings with Haig, Admiral Jorge Anaya of the junta said that Britain had no stomach for a fight, that democracies could not sustain casualties, and that the task force could not operate once winter came to the South Atlantic. On the third point, though certainly not on the first two, he was probably correct.

Mrs. Thatcher could, therefore, see no possibility of a peaceful solution in the days that the task force sailed south. She announced what she called a total exclusion zone two hundred nautical miles around the Falklands inside which any Argentine ships would be liable to being sunk without warning. Meanwhile, the chiefs of staff were warning the cabinet of possibly high losses and casualties, and even a possible 50 percent attrition rate in the latest addition to advanced military technology, Harrier Jump Jets. They also warned of the dangers posed by the French-made Exocet missiles that the Argentinians had recently bought. Fortunately, both Francis Pym and Willie Whitelaw had both won military crosses in the Second World War and were able to remind the rest of the war cabinet that part of the duty of chiefs of staff was to be excessively gloomy to politicians before battle was joined.

On April 25, South Georgia Island, which had also been invaded by Argentina, was liberated without loss by seventy-five Special Air Service (SAS), Special Boat Service (SBS), and Royal Marines. It required a direct attack, and afterward a bewildered Argentine officer complained to the SAS commander, "You've just walked through my minefield!"[13] In London, Mrs. Thatcher came out of No. 10 Downing Street and to the waiting press keen to ask questions she merely said, "Rejoice, just rejoice."[14]

Yet even at that crucial stage, not all Britons were rejoicing, or solidly supporting the use of force to liberate the Falklands, because they thought Mrs. Thatcher too bellicose and saw the United Nations as the ultimate arbiter for war and peace. A leading Labour Party politician, Tony Benn, and the Labour Party chairman campaigned against it and thirty-three Labour MPs voted against it in Parliament; the Trades Union Congress called on the government not to engage in military action; the three most senior figures in the Liberal Party stayed noticeably silent; the BBC featured a program on those Tories who were opposed to military action. A straw poll estimated that a majority of senior civil servants opposed sending the task force, including those in the Treasury, Foreign Office, and Cabinet Office. Most dangerously, Francis Pym was putting forward dovish views in the war cabinet while sounding hawkish in Parliament. (Margaret Thatcher took exquisite revenge on one occasion by asking him to defend to the full cabinet a controversial decision to which he had been adamantly opposed in the war cabinet.)

On the afternoon of May 1, the commander of the nuclear-powered submarine HMS *Conqueror* reported that he had sighted the 12,240-ton Argentine cruiser *General Belgrano*, which was escorted by two Exocet-armed destroyers, zigzagging in and out of the total exclusion zone. The *Belgrano* was providing aircraft direction for the Argentine air force and so posed a clear and present danger to any future British military operations on the islands. On the morning of May 2, Admiral Sir Terence Lewin went to the war cabinet meeting at the prime minister's country house, Chequers, to seek permission to sink her at once, even though at the time the *Belgrano* was some forty miles southwest of the zone. There was a full discussion and Mrs. Thatcher gave the order to sink her, with no minister dissenting. At some danger to herself, HMS *Conqueror* fired three Mark 8 torpedoes from two thousand yards at 3:00 P.M., two of which hit and sank the *Belgrano*, with the loss of 323 Argentine lives. It was the first major loss of life of the war and is still controversial today, but it demonstrated that the British were not bluffing and that, in the words of Hastings and Jenkins, "the seizure of the Falklands would be met by whatever level of force proved necessary to re-possess them."[15]

Later in the war there were British losses, such as the sinking of the type 42 destroyer HMS *Sheffield* by an Exocet missile launched from the air on May 4, the first Royal Navy vessel sunk in action since World War II. Twenty crew members were killed. (As the rest were waiting to be rescued from the ship after the attack, Sub-Lieutenant Carrington-Wood led the crew in singing the Monty Python song "Always Look on the Bright Side of Life.") On May 25—Argentina's national day—tremendously brave Argentine pilots attacking under heavy fire also sank HMS *Coventry*, with a further loss of twenty lives with twenty-nine wounded. These attacks left Margaret Thatcher visibly pained and desolate; on each occasion she retreated to her upstairs room at No. 10 and personally wrote letters in long-hand to the parents of each of the servicemen killed. In all, she had to write 255 such letters. "The Falklands marked her soul and mine," her husband, Denis, was to say.[16]

Yet for all the international, national, emotional, and media pressure on her, Mrs. Thatcher resolutely stuck to the cause of liberating the islands. She also refused to add to the pressure on the land commander on the spot, Lieutenant General Sir Julian Thompson, to break out early from the beachhead he had established at San Carlos Bay. On May 25, by which time five ships had been sunk, she told a group of Conservative women that "there can be no question of pressing the force commander to move forward prematurely."[17] When two days later Thompson did break out toward Stanley and Goose Green, she was relieved to be able to announce the fact to the House of Commons.

"Mrs Thatcher is under great pressure to get [Port] Stanley," a staff officer at the command unit at Northwood wrote in his diary at this time. "Every day that Stanley is not taken is another country lost to world opinion. We can't risk losing another ship or the Cabinet may not be able to resist pressure for a ceasefire."[18] There were several important battles to come, including the Battle of Goose Green and the night attack up Mount Tumbledown, the latter of which has been described as the toughest battle of the campaign. These and other such victories on the field led to the success that Margaret Thatcher and Admiral Leach had had the confidence to predict all those nerve-racking weeks earlier.

The Falklands taught Mrs. Thatcher that she needed her own office who could feed her information that she felt she was sometimes not receiving from departments of state, such as the Foreign Office and other ministries, which she felt distrusted her naturally combative instincts. "I'm jolly well realizing that I need a department," she said during the conflict. "I have no department and therefore I have to rely on third-hand hearsay, and I don't like it."[19] She had an inherent distaste for governmental "institutions" such as the Foreign Office, believing that they ossified thought, protected privilege, and removed incentive. Later she was to rely more on talented special advisers, people such as Sir Charles—later Lord—Powell, who she knew gave her independent advice largely unvarnished by the assumptions of the Foreign Office.

On Monday, June 14, at 10:15 P.M., the prime minister rose from her seat in the House of Commons to announce: "Our forces reached the outskirts of Port Stanley. Large numbers of Argentine soldiers threw down their weapons. They are reported to be flying white flags over Port Stanley."[20] The House of Commons erupted with cheers of relief and joy. Enoch Powell, who in the House of Commons debate at the start of the conflict had said that the conflict would show what mettle the Iron Lady was made of, told the House, "It shows that the substance under test consists of ferrous metal of the highest quality, that is of exceptional tensile strength, is highly resistant to wear and tear and to stress, and may be used with advantage for all national purposes."[21]

When she returned home to Downing Street that evening, exhausted but elated, Margaret Thatcher was kept awake by the crowds outside her door singing "Rule Britannia!" throughout the night. As the fleet returned to Portsmouth over the following days, vast crowds turned up to welcome home every ship, as towns and villages competed to honor their local servicemen and -women.

Her victory in the Falklands gave Mrs. Thatcher the confidence to take on the many nonmilitary challenges of her premiership. In the miners' strike of 1984–85, the aftermath of the assassination attempt on her by the IRA in October 1984, the demands for a rebate from Brussels's budgetary demands, the struggles over deregulation and denationalization, and her reaction to Saddam Hussein's invasion of Kuwait in August 1990, it is possible to discern the lesson of the Falklands War—that resolute action against antagonists solidified support far better than appeasement—being put into practice time and again.

"Today we meet in the aftermath of the Falklands Battle," Mrs. Thatcher said in a speech on July 3.

> Our country has won a great victory and we are entitled to be proud. This nation had the resolution to do what it knew had to be done—to do what it knew was right. We fought to show that aggression does not pay and that the robber cannot be allowed to get away with his swag. . . . We fought for our own people and for our own sovereign territory. Now that it is all over, things cannot be the same again for we have learned something about ourselves—a lesson which we desperately needed to learn. When we started out, there were the waverers and the fainthearts. . . . The people who thought we could no longer do the great things which we once did. Those who believed that our decline was irreversible—that we could never again be what we

were. There were those who would not admit it . . . people who would have strenuously denied the suggestion but—in their heart of hearts—they too had their secret fears that it was true: that Britain was no longer the nation that had built an Empire and ruled a quarter of the world. Well they were wrong. The lesson of the Falklands is that Britain has not changed and that this nation still has those sterling qualities which shine through our history. This generation can match their fathers and grandfathers in ability, in courage, and in resolution.[22]

It was true, and much of the credit for it must be put down to the ability, courage, resolution, and sheer leadership qualities of the most remarkable Englishwoman since Queen Elizabeth I.

THE LEADERSHIP
PARADIGM

T he story of the human race is war."[1] Winston Churchill's doleful conclusion has not been disproven since he made it in 1929; indeed, there has been only one year in the near three quarters of a century since the end of World War II when a British serviceman has not been killed on active duty somewhere in the world. (That year was 1966, over half a century ago.) Although arguments are made that the world has become a much safer place in recent years, not least by Professor Steven Pinker in his thought-provoking book about the decline of violence, *The Better Angels of Our Nature*, all it would take would be one miscalculation—or indeed one cynical calculation—to blow away all his encouraging statistics in the course of an afternoon.

The answer to this omnipresent blight on the human condition is a counterintuitive one; it is not to embrace pacifism and isolate oneself from the world and its troubles—the reach of the rocket and plane has become too great and the planet too interconnected for that to work anymore—but rather to do the precise opposite. The answer instead is to engage further and more actively in order to try to understand the phenomenon of war, the better to counteract its siren voice. This is not as hard as it first sounds, for as Churchill wrote to a Mr. J. H. Anderson in December 1906, thanking him for sending him an account of Sir John Moore's campaign in the Iberian Peninsula of 1808, "It is all one story in spite of every change in weapons; from the sheep under whose bellies Ulysses escaped from the cave of the Cyclops, to the oxen with which De Wet broke the blockhouse line in the Orange Free State."[2]*

Beside the desk in my study as I write this is a letter from Aldous Huxley written from Deronda Drive in Los Angeles in November 1959, which states, "That men do not learn very much from the lessons of history is the most important of the lessons that history has to teach us." Yet those few lessons we do learn must be the right ones. Out of the nine war leaders I have written about in this book, one remembered his school history teacher as a

---

* A reference to the Boer ambush of British forces at Waterval Drift on February 15, 1900, in the South African War.

---

grey-haired man whose fiery description made us forget the present and who evoked plain historical facts out of the fog of the centuries and turned them into living reality. [He] not only knew how to throw light on the past by utilizing the present, but also how to draw conclusions from the past and apply them to the present. More than anyone else he showed understanding for all the daily problems which held us breathless at the time. He was the teacher who made history my favourite subject.[3]

That was of course written by Adolf Hitler in *Mein Kampf* and illustrates how easy it has been for many people to learn the wrong lessons from history.

When one views the long story of the Ancient World up to and beyond the fall of the Roman Empire, it becomes clear that the commanders of the great Egyptian, Judean, Assyrian, Greek, Macedonian, Roman, and finally Hun empires provide not just examples of terrifying and inspiring leadership in themselves, but also the template for almost all the great commanders who came after them. It is impossible to consider the military and political career of Napoleon Bonaparte, for example, without appreciating how he consciously saw himself as a worthy modern successor to Alexander the Great and Julius Caesar, and he proved as much in his exile on the South Atlantic island of St. Helena, when he wrote Caesar's biography. It is likewise astounding how often battles like Cannae and Actium and leaders like Hannibal and Scipio crop up in the thought and conversation of the military leaders of the nineteenth and twentieth centuries. Eisenhower thought often about Cannae, as we have seen, and the battle is still taught at military academies today.[4]

Winston Churchill saw himself acting on the same historical plane as his great ancestor the duke of Marlborough and also of his other great hero, Napoleon. Besides them, his other templates for his leadership in 1940 were William Pitt the Younger in the Napoleonic Wars and David Lloyd George and Georges Clemenceau in the Great War. "Nelson's life should be a lesson to the youth of England," he wrote to his mother in December 1897.[5] Margaret Thatcher likewise drew her own inspiration during the Falklands War from Churchill. George Marshall's heroes were the giants of the American Civil War; as a young cadet at the Virginia Military Institute he had seen Stonewall Jackson's widow attend commemoration services there. Charles de Gaulle's heroes also included Clemenceau and, ironically enough as it turned out, Marshal Philippe Pétain, but they also went back to the great constables of France and to Joan of Arc, who repulsed the English. De Gaulle was curiously ambivalent about Napoleon, whom he thought of as a megalomaniac. (To which any Englishman must add: It takes one to know one.)

Stalin revered the distinctly unmilitary Karl Marx of course—as his latest biography by Stephen Kotkin confirms, far more than we even suspected—and not for nothing did

Hitler, who also admired Arminius, code-name his invasion of Russia after another of his heroes—Emperor Frederick I, known as Barbarossa.* You can thus tell a great deal about leaders from their heroes and their choice of historical moments from which they draw their inspiration.

As Cathal Nolan's brilliant recent book, *The Allure of Battle*, points out, leadership is not enough. Even the sheer panoply of leadership qualities that Napoleon showed in his career could not in the end save him and the First Empire. He was able to compartmentalize his mind, plan meticulously with a well-trained staff under Marshal Alexandre Berthier, appreciate terrain and guess what was on the other side of the hill, time his attacks perfectly, exhibit steady nerves to his entourage, encourage esprit de corps, publish inspirational proclamations, control the news cycle, adapt to modern tactical concepts, ask the right questions, and show utter ruthlessness when necessary. His charisma was not artificially created, and until the end he enjoyed remarkable runs of good luck. Above all, perhaps, he was single-minded in spotting the moment when he could exploit a numerical advantage at the decisive point on the battlefield.

Napoleon had all of these important leadership traits, but he still made the terrible error at Maloyaroslavets on October 25,

---

* Britain's field marshal Lord Inge told me that he had two great military maxims by which to guide himself, namely: "1. Never invade Russia," and "2. Never trust the RAF with your luggage."

1812, of choosing the wrong direction by which to take his army out of Russia. However generous the sprites and fairies are when they gather around the great leader's cradle with their gifts, there always seems to be a malicious one present to snatch back one gift from the cornucopia.

Churchill, too, had a panoply of leadership qualities. "Concentration was one of the keys to his character," recalled James Stuart, the government's chief whip. "It was not always obvious, but he never really thought of anything else but the job in hand."[6] Churchill melded his life entirely around his job during the Second World War, taking only eight days' proper holiday in the whole six years of conflict, six of those spent fishing in Canada and two swimming in Florida, but even on the latter trip he was attended by his red ministerial boxes and he read all the newspapers. Similarly, he was able to work almost throughout his two major bouts of pneumonia during the war.

Unsurprisingly, many other great leaders have also been workaholics—Margaret Thatcher, Helmuth von Moltke the Elder, and Marshal Ivan Konev are other examples. Of the nine in this book, only Hitler was genuinely lazy and lacked a proper work ethic. Energy is an almost demonic attribute, hard to characterize, and takes many forms. Churchill was one of the most energetic of all these leaders besides Napoleon, and yet he often did not get out of bed until noon—and that was for a hot bath—although he had been working hard on his papers since before breakfast.

A war leader's ability to plan meticulously is important,

despite Moltke's dictum that few plans last beyond the initial contact with the enemy. "Plans are worthless," agreed Eisenhower. "Planning is everything."[7] It is often forgotten that one of the most successful war plans in modern history—Hitler's blitzkrieg against the West that succeeded in knocking out France, Belgium, Luxembourg, and Holland in six weeks in May and June 1940—was not the original one. When the first set of plans fell into Allied hands by accident only days before the assault was due to be launched, Erich von Manstein drew up a new one. It was this plan B that featured the famous sickle-cut maneuver, in which concentrated armor cut the Allies off from their supply bases, the Maginot Line was skirted, the mountainous Ardennes forest—hitherto thought impassable—was used as a conduit, and the Germans broke through at Sedan in six days and reached the Channel coast at Abbeville in only ten. Few plan Bs in history have been so successful.

For planning in particular and for leadership in general a good memory is useful, or failing that an excellent filing system. Churchill had a phonographic memory, and not just for music-hall songs and Shakespeare. He would spend up to thirty hours memorizing his speeches and constantly practice them to make them word perfect, and would even make up ones he was not about to give but might be called upon to deliver sometime in the future. On occasion he would regale his entourage with speeches he would have given if he had been in the House of Commons at different periods of history. For a superb filing system one could hardly do better than Napoleon, who also had an excellent memory and who used his chief of staff, Marshal Alexandre Berthier, to ensure that even in a carriage rattling along at full pace they were able to place geographically every unit in his army and send and receive messages as aides-de-camps rode up to the windows, grasped orders thrust through the windows, and rode off again to deliver them.

Although it is impossible to quantify or predict, leaders need to be lucky as well as brilliant. Before he appointed anyone to the marshalate, Napoleon also wanted to know whether his generals were lucky, and luck undoubtedly does play a large part in war leadership. The role of chance and contingency in history is worthy of an entire book in itself and undermines the Whig, Marxist, and determinist theories of history in which mankind's progress is set on any definable tramlines.

The leader's capacity to appreciate terrain is not confined to the geographical and topographical. As Clausewitz famously put it, warfare is the continuation of politics by other means. A great leader also has to appreciate the political and economic terrain over which he is to campaign. Franklin Roosevelt might have wanted to bring the United States into World War II earlier than he eventually did—such was the isolationist sentiment at the time—but in the 1940 election he still had to make his promise in Boston to American parents that "your boys are not going to be sent into any foreign wars," in order to retain the White House and face the storm that was to come.[8] A leader has to be a realist, albeit one who appreciates the precise moment when it is possible to change public sentiment. In the event of course there was nothing foreign about the war that the Japanese unleashed on America in Hawaii on December 7, 1941. FDR had kept to the letter of his campaign promise.

In this area, Abraham Lincoln was also a supreme war leader, easily the equal of any of the nine in this book. His almost preternatural sense of what the Union would be able to accept politically, and when it would accept it, of what he could ask for and what he simply could not at any particular time, and his willingness to ride political storms, do necessary deals, sack underperforming or disloyal generals, and employ oratory of the Periclean quality of the Gettysburg Address and the two inaugural speeches, make him second to none as a war leader in the American pantheon.

"The reasonable man adapts himself to the world," wrote George Bernard Shaw in *Man and Superman*, "the unreasonable one persists in trying to adapt the world to himself. Therefore all progress depends on the unreasonable man." A talent for well-timed unreasonableness is another attribute of the great leader. Queen Elizabeth I refused to name her successor despite continual prompting from her Privy Council, thus protecting her country from the danger of civil war. Elizabeth I had many of the attributes of a great war leader, in her oratory, in her determination, and as a fine picker of men.

One thing that all these tribal leaders have in common— except Hitler at the very end who came to hate the German people and wanted to punish them with the "Nero Order" for failing his Nazi ideals by losing—was an absolute faith in their tribes' being superior to their antagonists. Churchill's and Thatcher's view of Englishness, de Gaulle's "certain idea of France" (which uncannily mirrored Napoleon's, even though Corsica had become French only the year before his birth), Abraham Lincoln's and both Roosevelts' belief in America as the most extraordinary experiment in nation-creating in human history—all of them believed in the capabilities of the tribe he or she led. They believed in what is now called national exceptionalism, as tribal leaders throughout history have—look at Pericles's view of Athens in the funeral speech or Bismarck's "Iron and Blood" speech.

A sense of humor is not necessary in a great commander. Margaret Thatcher, much as she is admired for her other qualities, had none whatsoever, and it was said that Helmuth von Moltke the Elder smiled only twice in his life: the first time when someone suggested that the fortress of Liège was too strong to be captured, and the second when he was told that his mother-in-law had died. Nonetheless, Churchill and Napoleon and Lincoln all had fine senses of humor, able to charm the nations they led as well as inspire them.

Having steady nerves in a crisis cannot be underestimated, but can be learned. Basil Liddell Hart wrote in his 1944 book *Thoughts on War* that "the two qualities of mental initiative and strong personality, or determination, go a long way towards the power of command in war—they are, indeed, the hallmark of the Great Captains."[9] Although Stalin had something approaching a mental breakdown when he heard about Operation

Barbarossa on June 22, 1941, retiring to his dacha for days as the Red Army and Air Force were pounded on every front, by mid-October, when the Germans were at the gates of Moscow, his nerves had steadied enough for him to stay and fight it out. Charles de Gaulle's behavior on August 26, 1944, when he attended the service of liberation in Notre-Dame while bullets were being fired within the cathedral itself, also showed rock-steady nerves. Margaret Thatcher during the Falklands crisis and after the IRA assassination attempt on her in October 1984, and Churchill throughout World War II, showed similarly complete self-control in crises, just as Napoleon had when his army retreated during the early stages of the Battle of Marengo. Such calm under pressure is the very quintessence of leadership.

An appreciation of the importance of discipline and training was central to the war leadership of Generals Marshall and Eisenhower, the scale of whose achievements is still awe inspiring three quarters of a century later. To have trained an army up from virtually nothing—the fourteenth-largest in the world, equal to Romania's—to be in a position by the time of D-Day only two and a half years later to take on the best of the Wehrmacht and win in open country, was a truly extraordinary achievement. Discipline had to be imposed on generals as well as on men—no one sacked as many generals in American history as did George Marshall, and even Patton had to be severely disciplined by Eisenhower after the face-slapping incident. Training was the watchword of both Marshall and Eisenhower, who struck precisely the right balance between eliminating slackness and allowing their generals to retain initiative. Nelson's years at sea were spent in regular gunnery training, and Napoleon ensured that when the Grande Armée was stationed at the Channel ports in 1803–5 it took part in endless maneuvers to prepare them for the battles to come.

In October 1944 Patton defined leadership as a capacity for "telling somebody who thinks he is beaten that he is not beaten."[10] As wars are won by the victor of the last battle, the capacity for inspiring the losers of the penultimate battle is key. Here, the sheer doggedness of George Washington stands out supreme, alongside that of Churchill in 1940. Aside from the evacuation from Brooklyn across the East River in August 1776—where a weird combination of low mist and adverse wind direction somehow prevented the Royal Navy from scooping up a force that was down to only nine thousand—Washington enjoyed few successes in 1775 and 1776. As Churchill said of Dunkirk, "Wars are not won by evacuations," but, also like Dunkirk, the sheer fact of survival and escape was in itself a victory for the American revolutionaries. Simply surviving the hardships of Valley Forge through the winter kept the cause alive and could not have been achieved without George Washington's shining leadership by personal example. What Liddell Hart called "mental initiative and strong personality, or determination," was personified by Washington in that freezing winter of 1776–77, and was exhibited by all the other leaders in this book. Except through heredity, one does not become a war leader in the first place unless one has a strong personality.

Understanding the psychology of both the ordinary soldier and the civilian is an important part of war leadership. Today it seems to be assumed that in order to lead one's people one needs to have sprung from them, but that is not the case. Many of those who have exuded leadership ability hailed from the leisured or moneyed class of their countries—Alexander the Great, Julius Caesar, Napoleon, Churchill, both Roosevelts, and John F. Kennedy among a long list of them—yet they all had a strong sense of what motivated soldiers and citizens who hailed from backgrounds far further down the social scale. A capacity to empathize is far more important than one's class background. Churchill was born in a palace the grandson of a duke, went to one of the top schools in the country, and never took a bus in his life, but he could speak directly to the needs of what he called "the cottage home." When commanding in the trenches of the Great War, he put his earlier campaigning experience to good use in always trying to ensure the men had their creature comforts, such as beer, fresh bread, and a good postal service to connect them with their families.

Napoleon similarly learned from Caesar the manner by which men could be shamed into showing bravery. He admonished troops whom he considered to have fallen below expectations, as in the Italian campaign of 1796–97. In his book *Napoleon's Commentaries on the Wars of Julius Caesar,* Napoleon recounted the story of a mutiny in Rome when Caesar had laconically agreed to his soldiers' demands to be demobilized, but then addressed them with ill-concealed contempt as "citizens" rather than "soldiers" or "comrades." "The result of this moving scene was to win the continuation of their services," Napoleon noted.[11]

In order for this to work, the leader needs to have displayed a personal courage that is admired by his or her followers and spoken of years after the event. Nelson lost an eye and an arm in battle; Napoleon fought sixty battles, was wounded twice, and survived numerous assassination attempts with aplomb; Stalin showed some bravery as a serial bank robber, and refused to get on his personal train to leave Moscow on October 18, 1941. Hitler won the Iron Cross first class and second class (although it has been discovered recently that the medals went to all the runners in the 16th Bavarian Reserve Regiment, regardless of personal bravery).

Charles de Gaulle was involved in so much close fighting in World War I that he was famed throughout the French Army for his courage. Of those who for various reasons did not have the opportunity to see combat, George Marshall and Dwight Eisenhower were on the staffs and no one doubts that they would have shown courage if they had had the opportunity; Margaret Thatcher held herself with tremendous calm, courage, and dignity when the IRA attempted to assassinate her.

Surprisingly, a capacity for great oratory is not absolutely indispensable for leadership—Napoleon was not much of a public speaker, for example—but it can be extraordinarily helpful. Great leaders take care not to let the military establishments and staffs get between them and those they are leading, and to be able to speak directly to one's followers is thus invaluable. Every method possible has been used to close that gap, from Napoleon's Orders of the Day and proclamations to the Grande Armée to Second World War generals standing up in jeeps to address individual units. Although it is fashionable to decry President Trump's present-day use of Twitter to communicate directly with the electorate, it is a device that would probably have been used by most leaders if they had been able. Napoleon's christening of one of his batteries at Toulon "Les Hommes sans Peur" (Men Without Fear) showed a capacity to say what he needed to in 280 characters or fewer. Indeed, his phrase to his troops before the Battle of the Pyramids—"Forty centuries look down upon you"—has all the makings of an excellent short tweet.

"Leadership is more than technique, though techniques are necessary," Richard Nixon wrote in his book *Leaders*. "In a sense, management is prose; leadership is poetry. The leader necessarily deals to a large extent in symbols, in images, and in the sort of galvanizing idea that becomes a force of history. People are persuaded by reason, but moved by emotion."[12] One of the emotions that leaders must occasionally inspire is fear, and acts of ruthlessness are part and parcel of war leadership. Napoleon's massacre of the Turkish artillerymen after the capture of Jaffa in 1799 was a case in point, as was Nelson's execution of Commodore Francesco Caracciolo. The duke of Wellington's scorched-earth policy outside Lisbon—committed on the territory of Britain's ally Portugal—was ruthless, as was William

Tecumseh Sherman's march to the sea in the Savannah campaign of late 1864. Churchill's moments of ruthlessness came when he sank the French fleet at Oran, bullied the Polish government in London into recognizing the Communist Lublin Polish government, and agreed at Yalta to ship tens of thousands of Cossacks who had fought for Hitler back to the Soviet Union, where they faced almost certain death.

Sun Tzu famously remarked in rule 2 of chapter 3 of *The Art of War*, "Hence to fight and conquer in all your battles is not supreme excellence; supreme excellence consists in breaking the enemy's resistance without fighting."[13] Great leaders create a reputation for invincibility for themselves, thereby overawing their opponents. This capacity for propaganda and image creation can clearly be seen in the careers of Thutmose III, King Ashurbanipal of Assyria, Alcibiades, Pompey, Trajan, Genghis and Kublai Khan, Hernán Cortés, Akbar the Great, Gustavus Adolphus, Erwin Rommel, Bernard Montgomery, George Patton, and Moshe Dayan, as well as several of the leaders in this book who carefully curated their reputations for invincibility, such as Napoleon, Nelson, and Hitler. They recognized that if their reputations could help conquer, and thus save the lives of their men, who were they to be modest? The number of genuinely modest or retiring great commanders is few, but might include Ulysses Grant, Dwight Eisenhower, George Marshall, and Sir William Slim.

Perhaps surprisingly there is some overlap between successful war leadership and literary ability, quite beyond the capacity for propaganda, though this might just reflect the overlap between successful leadership and high intellect. Julius Caesar, Xenophon, Frederick the Great, Napoleon, Grant in his memoirs, and David Lloyd George all showed at least some literary talent. Although he did not of course survive to write his memoirs, Lord Nelson, like Churchill, could scarcely write a dull sentence, and when he was describing a battle scene he breathlessly brought his readers right into the action. Here he is writing on HMS *Agamemnon*, describing to a comrade his attack on the French in Corsica in February 1794:

> No sooner did we get within reach, than they began at us, with Shot & Shells. I back'd our Main topsail that we might be as long as possible in passing & return'd their fire for one hour & [a] half when we were drawing to too great a distance for our shot to do execution. The fire from the Ships was well kept up, & I am sure that not ten shot [were] fired which did not do Service, on one battery a vast explosion of gunpowder took place, and it was some time before they could extinguish it. The Enemy's fire was very badly directed, each Ship had a few shot struck her, but not a Man killed or wounded.[14]

If Nelson had somehow failed as a sailor, he could have made a decent living as a novelist of his wars, predating C. S. Forester,

Patrick O'Brian, and Bernard Cornwell. Considering that Nelson left school to become a midshipman just short of his thirteenth birthday, it is a tribute to the education available on late-eighteenth-century Royal Navy vessels that he was as literate as he was. The only moment when his grammar completely broke down was when he fell into the throes of furious sexual jealousy, believing the Prince of Wales was trying to seduce Lady Hamilton in 1801. His longing for her is worthy of the metaphysical poets, writing: "Even had I Millions or an Empire you should participate it with Me."[15]

As Nelson knew, the capacity to launch a surprise attack and then retain the initiative has always been important in warfare, from the career of Joshua in the thirteenth century B.C. to that of General Giap in the 1960s. Surprises have included Hannibal taking elephants across the Alps in 218 B.C.—a route Napoleon also took for his surprise attack that led to the Battle of Marengo in 1800—all the way to Gerd von Rundstedt's attack through the Ardennes that led to the Battle of the Bulge in December 1944, and beyond. Indeed, Paul Wolfowitz, the former U.S. deputy secretary of defense, said at his commencement address at the West Point Military Academy graduation in June 2001, "Surprise happens so often that it's surprising that we're surprised by it."

Because war is indeed, as Carl von Clausewitz put it, the continuation of politics by other means, it is vital for the war leaders to have a sixth sense for politics, which in some areas is similar to military skill, such as in the importance of having a feel for the coup d'oeil, a sense of timing, an aptitude for observation, the gift of working out what is genuinely important as opposed to merely diversionary, a faculty for predicting an opponent's likely behavior in differing scenarios. Here one must commend the politicomilitary thinking of Ramses II, King David, Charlemagne, William the Conqueror, Sultan Mehmet II, Süleyman the Magnificent, Frederick the Great, Clive of India, Simón Bolívar, Kemal Atatürk, Carl Gustaf Mannerheim, and Gerald Templer. Of course opportunism played a large part in the success of many of these political generals and commander-politicians. "A statesman must," in Otto von Bismarck's phrase, "wait and listen until he hears the steps of God sounding through events; then leap up and grasp the hem of His garment."[16]

There are many great military commanders who by contrast got the military side right but the political disastrously wrong, and one might include Xenophon, Pompey, Robert E. Lee, and Stonewall Jackson; Erich Ludendorff after World War I as well of course as Gerd von Rundstedt, Erich von Manstein, and Heinz Guderian in World War II. Philippe Pétain was a great military leader in World War I and a disastrous political one in World War II. Even Thucydides himself was exiled. Sometimes military and political leadership do go together—as with Dwight Eisenhower—but they are not so connected as to have the automatic crossover one might expect.

Leadership has scarcely ever been better exemplified than during the—unsuccessful as it turned out—visit of Winston

Churchill to Briaire on the afternoon of Wednesday, June 12, 1940. He had landed at a small airfield near the town on the Loire about fifty miles east of Orléans the previous day for a supreme war council with the French premier, Paul Reynaud, where the French commander in chief, General Maxime Weygand, along with Marshal Pétain, had set out the dire facts of the German breakthroughs in the northwest of France. Indeed, Paris was to fall three days later. Charles de Gaulle was there, too, only days away from flying to London and making his seminal broadcast.

After Weygand explained the plight of the French Army, he exclaimed: "Here is the decisive point [*point d'appui*]. Now is the decisive moment. The British ought not to keep a single fighter in England. They should all be sent to France."[17] At this there was an awful pause, and Churchill's advisers feared lest his generosity, Francophilia, courage, and optimism should move him to promise more air support—despite fighter command's commander in chief Air Chief Marshal Sir Hugh Dowding having warned him that if any more fighter squadrons were sent to France he could no longer guarantee the defense of the British Isles.

After a pause, and speaking very slowly, Churchill flatly contradicted Weygand, saying,

> This is not the decisive point. This is not the decisive moment. The decisive moment will come when Hitler hurls his Luftwaffe against Britain. If we can keep the

command of the air over our own island—that is all I
ask—then we will win it all back for you. . . . Whatever
happens here, we are resolved to fight on for ever and
ever and ever.[18]

The next morning there were further meetings at which it
was agreed that Britain would send over divisions to try to organize a defensive redoubt in Brittany. Meanwhile, against their
own promises and clearly preparing to surrender, the French
prevented the RAF in the south of France from bombing Italian targets only forty-eight hours after Mussolini had joined
the war on Hitler's side. As they reached the airfield on the way
home, General Sir Hastings (Pug) Ismay, Churchill's military
secretary, pleaded that because the divisions being sent would
certainly have to be evacuated, and might well be captured,
could the British government not unobtrusively delay their departure? "Certainly not," replied Churchill. "It would look very
bad in history if we were to do any such thing."[19]

The troops were dispatched. The Germans could not be
stopped, and 191,870 men of the Second British Expeditionary
Force were indeed evacuated in a smaller, less famous version of
Dunkirk. But the effort had been made, Britain's side of the bar-
gain had been honored, even while France's was not being. Great
war leader that he was, Churchill was not looking to the immediate judgment of the press, or Parliament, or even the public for
his vindication, but to the ages, to what he memorably called on
a later occasion "the grievous inquest of History."[20] In a sense

he was looking for the approval of people as yet unborn, the kind of people who meet to discuss such matters in historical societies and read books of essays on such topics three quarters of a century later. In a word: us. That was where he was looking for his vindication, and where I hope that he has found it.

It would be easy to say that, like the rhinoceros, leadership is hard to define from first principles but you certainly recognize it when you see it. Yet in fact there are certain definable principles and leadership techniques that are eternal, as applicable to Cyrus the Great and Leonidas as to Georgy Zhukov and Sir Gerald Templer. What is more, they can be learned, which is why the careers and battles of some of the great military commanders of the past are rightly still taught at naval and military academies such as West Point, Annapolis, Sandhurst, St. Cyr, and Shrivenham today.

Reviewing Alfred Duff Cooper's biography of Field Marshal Earl Haig in the *Daily Mail* in October 1935, Churchill wrote that "no one can discern a spark of that mysterious, visionary, often sinister genius which has enabled the great captains of history to dominate the material factors, save slaughter, and confront their foes with the triumph of novel apparitions."[21] Haig certainly failed in those three—he could not dominate the material factors of trenches and flat ground and the machine gun, nor save slaughter, and without Churchill's godfathering the tank there would have been virtually no novel apparitions on the battlefield except for poison gas, which was first used by the Germans. Trenches, machine guns, and railways had already all been seen in the American Civil War half a century earlier. This book has been about that "mysterious, visionary, often sinister genius" that differentiates the Haigs—who do their best under appalling circumstances—from the great commanders.

If you want to know what will move hearts and command multitudes today and in the future, there is only one thing to do: Study the past. In May 1953 Churchill said, "Study history. Study history. In history lie all the secrets of statecraft," and the same is true of statecraft's vital subsection, war leadership.[22] If there is one quality that all the great war leaders possessed, it is that which the earl of St. Vincent ascribed to Horatio Nelson. St. Vincent did not much like his fellow admiral personally, but he readily admitted that Nelson "possessed the magic art of infusing his own spirit into others."[23] Great leaders are able to make soldiers and civilians believe that they are part of a purpose that matters more than even their continued existence on the planet, and that the leader's spirit is infused into them. Whether it is a "magic art" or "sinister genius" can be decided by moralists, but in it lies the secret of successful leadership in war.

ACKNOWLEDGMENTS

These short pen portraits started life as lectures that I delivered to the New-York Historical Society as the Lehrman Institute Distinguished Lecturer between 2014 and 2018, thanks to the splendid generosity of Lewis E. Lehrman and his wife, Louise, to whom this book is dedicated. I would like to acknowledge their many great kindnesses to me both then and since, and also the hospitality and friendship of the New-York Historical Society's chair Pam Schafler, president and CEO Louise Mirrer, staff members Dale Gregory and Alex Kassl, as well as many others in that wonderful place where I have hugely enjoyed so many evenings over the years, and continue to as their Lehrman Institute Distinguished Lecturer on Sir Winston Churchill.

Much of the additional work on this book was done at the Hoover Institution at Stanford in my capacity as a visiting research fellow, thanks to the great generosity of Roger and Martha Mertz. I would also like to acknowledge them with gratitude, as well as the diligence of Yasmin Samrai in tracking down all the endnote references.

Andrew Roberts
April 2019

NOTES

CHAPTER ONE: NAPOLEON BONAPARTE

1. Winston S. Churchill, *A History of the English-Speaking Peoples*, vol. 3, *The Age of Revolution* (London: Bloomsbury Academic, 1957), 225.
2. Digby Smith, *1813 Leipzig: Napoleon and the Battle of the Nations* (London: Greenhill Books, 2001), 189.
3. Andrew Uffindell, *Napoleon's Immortals: The Imperial Guard and Its Battles, 1804–1815* (London: Spellmount Publishers, 2007), 245.
4. Philip J. Haythornthwaite, *Napoleon: The Final Verdict* (London: Arms and Armour Press, 1996), 220.
5. Baron de Marbot, *The Exploits of Baron de Marbot*, ed. Christopher Summerville (New York: Carroll & Graf, 2000), 137.
6. Baron Louis François de Bausset-Roquefort, *Private Memoirs of the Court of Napoleon* (Philadelphia: Carey, Lea & Carey, 1828), 67.
7. George Bourne, *The History of Napoleon Bonaparte* (Baltimore: Warner & Hanna, 1806), 376.
8. Duchess D'Abrantès, *At the Court of Napoleon* (Gloucester, UK: The Windrush Press, 1991), 117.
9. Napoleon, *Correspondance Générale*, vol. 4, *Ruptures et fondation 1803–1804*, ed. François Houdecek, letter no. 8731, March 12, 1804 (Paris: Éditions Fayard, 2007), 637–38.
10. General Count Philip [Philippe] de Ségur, *History of the Expedition to Russia*, vol. 1 (London: Thomas Tegg, 1840), 182.

11. Baron Ernst von Odeleben, *A Circumstantial Narrative of the Campaign in Saxony in 1813* (London: John Murray, 1820), 182.

12. Ibid., 183.

13. Henry Houssaye, *The Return of Napoleon* (London: Longmans, Green and Co., 1934), 7.

14. Bausset-Roquefort, *Private Memoirs of the Court of Napoleon*, 67.

15. Jean-Antoine Chaptal, *Mes souvenirs de Napoléon* (Paris: E. Plon, Nourrit et Cie, 1893), 337.

16. Lieut.-Gen. Count Mathieu Dumas, *Memoirs of His Own Time*, vol. 2 (Philadelphia: Lea & Blanchard, 1839), 223.

17. Ibid., 107.

18. Richard Henry Horne, *The History of Napoleon*, vol. 1 (London: Robert Tyas, 1841), 153.

19. John H. Gill, *With Eagles to Glory: Napoleon and His German Allies in the 1809 Campaign* (London: Greenhill Books, 1992), 9.

20. David Chandler, *The Military Maxims of Napoleon* (New York: Macmillan, 1987), 203.

21. Haythornthwaite, *Napoleon: The Final Verdict*, 222.

22. Kevin Kiley, *Once There Were Titans: Napoleon's Generals and Their Battles* (London: Greenhill Books, 2007), 19.

23. William Francklyn Paris, *Napoleon's Legion* (London: Funk and Wagnalls Co., 1927), 15.

24. Napoleon, *Correspondance de Napoléon Ier*, ed. Henri Plon, vol. 32 (Paris: Imprimerie Impériale, 1858), 68.

25. David Chandler, *On the Napoleonic Wars: Collected Essays* (London: Greenhill Books, 1994), 99.

26. Michael Hughes, *Forging Napoleon's Grande Armée* (New York: New York University Press, 2012), 25.

27. Antoine-Henri, Baron de Jomini, *Summary of the Art of War* (New York: G. P. Putnam & Co., 1854), 73.

28. Ibid.

29. David Johnson, *Napoleon's Cavalry and Its Leaders* (New York: Holmes & Meier, 1978), 22.

30. Chandler, *On the Napoleonic Wars*, 114.

31. Haythornthwaite, *Napoleon: The Final Verdict*, 224.

32. Léon de Lanzac de Laborie, *Paris sous Napoleon*, vol. 2 (Paris: Librairie Plon, 1905), 92.

33. Marquis de Noailles, ed., *The Life and Memoirs of Count Molé*, vol. 1 (London: Hutchinson, 1923), 163.

34. Fondation Napoleon, *Correspondance Générale*, vol. 9, *Wagram, Février 1809—Février 1810*, ed. Patrice Gueniffey, letter no. 20869 (Paris: Éditions Fayard, 2013), 510.

35. Nigel Nicolson, *Napoleon: 1812* (New York: HarperCollins, 1985), 99.

CHAPTER TWO: HORATIO NELSON

1. Letter from Benjamin Disraeli to Queen Victoria, August 24, 1879, from William Flavelle Monypenny and George Earle Buckle, *The Life of Benjamin Disraeli, Earl of Beaconsfield*, vol. 6 (New York: Macmillan, 1920), 435.

2. E. Hallam Moorhouse, "Nelson as Seen in His Letters," *Fortnightly Review*, ed. W. L. Courtney, vol. 96, 1911, 718.

3. Horatio Nelson, "Sketch of His Life," October 15, 1799, from Nicholas Harris Nicolas, ed., *The Dispatches and Letters of Vice Admiral Lord Viscount Nelson*, vol. 1, *1777–1794* (London: Henry Colburn, 1844), 15.

4. John Sugden, *Nelson: A Dream of Glory, 1758–1797* (New York: Henry Holt and Co., 2004), 105.

5. Ibid.

6. Ibid., 121.

7. Ibid., 217.

8. Robert Southey, *The Life of Horatio, Lord Nelson* (London: J. M. Dent & Sons, 1902), 131.

9. Terry Coleman, *The Nelson Touch: The Life and Legend of Horatio Nelson* (New York: Oxford University Press, 2002), 124.

10. Ibid., 147.

11. John Sugden, *Nelson: The Sword of Albion* (New York: Henry Holt and Co., 2013), 127.
12. Coleman, *The Nelson Touch*, 7.
13. Ibid., 18.
14. Tom Pocock, "Nelson, Not by Halves," *The Times* (London), July 23, 1996.
15. Southey, *The Life of Horatio, Lord Nelson*, 327.
16. Letter from Nelson to Lady Hamilton, September 17, 1805, from *The Living Age*, vol. 12, 1847, 140.
17. Letter from Nelson to Lady Hamilton, April 28, 1804, from Thomas Joseph Pettigrew, *Memoirs of the Life of Vice-Admiral Lord Viscount Nelson*, vol. 2 (London: T. & W. Boone, 1849), 390.
18. Letter from Nelson to Lord Barham, October 5, 1805, from James Stanier Clarke and John M'Arthur, *The Life of Admiral Lord Nelson from His Manuscripts*, vol. 2 (London: Bensley, 1809), 431.
19. Nelson at the Battle of Trafalgar, October 21, 1805, quoted in Nicholas Harris Nicolas, ed., *The Dispatches and Letters of Vice Admiral Lord Viscount Nelson*, vol. 7, *August to October 1805* (London: Henry Colburn, 1846), 14.
20. Coleman, *The Nelson Touch*, 261.
21. Sugden, *Nelson: The Sword of Albion*, 827–28.
22. Ibid., 832.

CHAPTER THREE: WINSTON CHURCHILL

1. Private diary entry of King George VI, May 10, 1940, Royal Archives, Windsor Castle.
2. Walter Thompson, *I Was Churchill's Shadow* (London: Christopher Johnson, 1951), 37.
3. Lord Moran, *Winston Churchill: The Struggle for Survival* (London: Constable & Co., 1966), 324.
4. Ibid.

5. Winston S. Churchill, *The Second World War*, vol. 1, *The Gathering Storm* (Boston: Houghton Mifflin, 1948), 526–27.
6. A. G. Gardiner, *Pillars of Society* (London: J. M. Dent, 1913), 61.
7. Martin Gilbert, *In Search of Churchill* (New York: HarperCollins, 1994), 215.
8. Winston S. Churchill, *Great Contemporaries*, ed. James W. Muller (Wilmington, DE: ISI Books, 2012), 235.
9. David Reynolds, *Summits: Six Meetings That Shaped the Twentieth Century* (New York: Basic Books, 2007), 57. See also Neville to Ida, September 19, 1938, Neville Chamberlain Papers 18/11/1069, The National Archives: The Cabinet Office Papers.
10. Churchill, *The Gathering Storm*, vol. 1, 75.
11. Winston Churchill, *The River War*, vol. 1 (London: Longmans, Green and Co., 1899), 37.
12. Anthony Montague Browne, *Long Sunset: Memoirs of Winston Churchill's Last Private Secretary* (London: Cassell, 1995), 119.
13. Hastings Lionel Ismay, *The Memoirs of Lord Ismay* (New York: Viking Press, 1960), 183–84.
14. Winston S. Churchill, *Winston Churchill: Thoughts and Adventures*, ed. James W. Muller (Wilmington, DE: ISI Books, 2009), 9.
15. Winston Churchill, "A Second Choice," in Churchill, *Thoughts and Adventures*, 10.
16. Letter from Winston to Clementine, in *Speaking for Themselves: The Personal Letters of Winston and Clementine Churchill*, ed. Mary Soames (New York: Doubleday, 1999), 149.
17. John Colville, *The Fringes of Power: Downing Street Diaries, 1939–1955* (New York: W. W. Norton & Co., 1986), 432–33.
18. James Leasor, *War at the Top* (London: Michael Joseph, 1959), 148n1.
19. House of Commons Debate, June 15, 1944, *Hansard*, vol. 400, cc2293–2300.

CHAPTER FOUR: ADOLF HITLER

1. Adolf Hitler, *Hitler's Table Talk, 1941–44: His Private Conversations*, ed. Hugh Trevor-Roper (New York: Enigma Books, 2007), 356.
2. Ibid., 443.
3. Ibid., 233.
4. Ibid., 682–83.
5. Ibid., 241.
6. Ibid., 245.
7. Ibid., 126.
8. Ibid., 252.
9. Ibid., 359.
10. Ibid., 360.
11. Ibid., 188.
12. Ibid., 397.
13. Ibid., 545.
14. Ibid., 236.
15. Ibid., 249.
16. Ibid., 250.
17. Ibid., 195.
18. Ibid., 194.
19. Adolf Hitler, *Mein Kampf* (Boston: Houghton Mifflin, 1998), 289.
20. Laurence Rees, *The Holocaust: A New History* (New York: PublicAffairs, 2017), 59.
21. Ian Kershaw, *Hitler: A Biography* (New York: W. W. Norton & Co., 2008), 562.
22. Hitler, *Hitler's Table Talk*, 241.
23. Kershaw, *Hitler*, 649.
24. Adolf Hitler, speech on Stalingrad, September 30, 1942, in Laurence Rees, *Hitler's Charisma: Leading Millions into the Abyss* (New York: Pantheon Books, 2012), 268.
25. Hitler, *Hitler's Table Talk*, 145.
26. Ibid., 79.

27. Ibid., 87.
28. Ibid., 332.
29. Hitler, speech before the Reichsleiters and Gauleiters, August 4, 1944, in Max Domarus, *The Essential Hitler: Speeches and Commentary*, ed. Patrick Romane (Wauconda, IL: Bolchazy-Carducci Publishers, 2007), 791.
30. Hitler, *Hitler's Table Talk*, 196.
31. Ferenc A. Vajda and Peter G. Dancey, *German Aircraft Industry and Production: 1933–1945* (Warrendale, PA: Society of Automotive Engineers, 1998), 101.
32. Adolf Hitler's marriage license, April 29, 1945, William Russell Philip collection (Box 9, Item 7), Hoover Institution Library and Archives.

CHAPTER FIVE: JOSEPH STALIN

1. Alan Bullock, *Hitler and Stalin: Parallel Lives* (New York: Harper-Collins, 1991), 511.
2. Simon Sebag Montefiore, *Stalin: The Court of the Red Tsar* (New York: Vintage Books, 2003), 219.
3. Joseph Stalin, "Morning," quoted in Robert Service, *Stalin: A Biography* (Cambridge, MA: Harvard University Press, 2005), 38.
4. Stephen Kotkin, *Stalin*, vol. 1, *Paradoxes of Power, 1878–1928* (New York: Penguin Books, 2014), 8–9.
5. Joseph Stalin, "Industrialisation and the Grain Problem," July 9, 1928, quoted in Evan Mawdsley, *The Stalin Years: The Soviet Union, 1929–1953* (Manchester, UK: Manchester University Press, 1998), 120.
6. Kotkin, *Stalin: Paradoxes of Power*, 732.
7. Robert Gellately, *Stalin's Curse: Battling for Communism in War and Cold War* (New York: Vintage Books, 2013), 7.
8. Joseph Stalin, "Report on the Work of the Central Committee to the Eighteenth Congress of the C.P.S.U. (B.)," March 10, 1939, in J. V. Stalin, *Works, 1939–1940*, vol. 14 (London: Red Star Press, 1978).

9. Service, *Stalin*, 410.

10. Ibid., 411.

11. Ibid., 421.

12. Ibid.

13. Lewis E. Lehrman, *Churchill, Roosevelt & Company: Studies in Character and Statecraft* (Mechanicsburg, PA: Stackpole Books, 2017), 6.

14. Amos Perlmutter, *FDR & Stalin: A Not So Grand Alliance, 1943–1945* (Columbia: University of Missouri, 1993), 139.

15. Service, *Stalin*, 428.

16. Ibid., 454.

17. Albert Axell, *Stalin's War: Through the Eyes of His Commanders* (London: Arms and Armour Press, 1997), 139.

18. Frank Roberts, quoted in foreword by Arthur M. Schlesinger, Jr., in Susan Butler, ed., *My Dear Mr. Stalin: The Complete Correspondence of Franklin D. Roosevelt and Joseph V. Stalin* (New Haven: Yale University Press, 2005), x.

19. Letter from Roosevelt to Churchill, March 18, 1942, in Warren F. Kimball, ed., *Churchill and Roosevelt: The Complete Correspondence*, vol. 1 (Princeton, NJ: Princeton University Press, 2015), 420–21.

20. Richard Overy, "A Curious Correspondence," review of *My Dear Mr. Stalin*, ed. Susan Butler, *Literary Review*, May 2006, 20–21.

21. Butler, *My Dear Mr. Stalin*, 280.

22. Letter from Roosevelt to Stalin, January 25, 1943, in Butler, *My Dear Mr. Stalin*, 113.

23. Montefiore, *Stalin: The Court of the Red Tsar*, 43.

24. Antony Beevor, *The Second World War* (New York: Hachette, 2012), 689.

25. Kotkin, *Stalin: Paradoxes of Power*, 735.

26. Raymond Carr, "The Nature of the Beast," review of *Stalin* by Robert Service in *The Spectator*, December 4, 2004.

CHAPTER SIX: GEORGE C. MARSHALL

1. Letter from Mrs. to Mr. Churchill, in *Speaking for Themselves: The Personal Letters of Winston and Clementine*, ed. Mary Soames (New York: Doubleday, 1999), 546.

2. Ibid.

3. Ibid., 548.

4. Roger Daniels, *Franklin D. Roosevelt: The War Years, 1939–1945* (Champaign: University of Illinois Press, 2016), 373.

5. Katherine Tupper Marshall, *Together: Annals of an Army Wife* (New York: Tupper & Love, Inc., 1946), 110.

6. Katherine Tupper Marshall, *Together: Annals of an Army Wife* (New York: Tupper and Love, 1946), 110.

7. Albert C. Wedemeyer, *Wedemeyer Reports!* (New York: Henry Holt, 1958), 132.

8. Ibid., 105.

9. Ibid., 132.

10. Ibid., 133.

11. Ibid., 134.

12. Franklin D. Roosevelt, memorandum to Marshall, July 16, 1942, quoted in Winston S. Churchill, *The Hinge of Fate* (London: Weidenfeld & Nicolson, 2001), 399.

13. Lewis E. Lehrman, *Churchill, Roosevelt & Company: Studies in Character and Statecraft* (Mechanicsburg, PA: Stackpole Books, 2017), 70.

14. Field Marshal Lord Alanbrooke, *War Diaries 1939–1945*, ed. Alex Danchev and Daniel Todman (Berkeley: University of California Press, 2003), 680.

15. Martin Gilbert, *Winston S. Churchill*, vol. 7, *Road to Victory, 1941–1945* (Boston: Houghton Mifflin, 1986), 843.

16. Churchill, *The Hinge of Fate*, 344.

CHAPTER SEVEN: CHARLES DE GAULLE

1. Jean Lacouture, *De Gaulle: The Rebel 1890–1944*, vol. 1 (New York: W. W. Norton & Co., 1990), 220.
2. Julian Jackson, *De Gaulle* (Cambridge, MA: Belknap Press, 2018), 48, 58.
3. Ibid., 132.
4. Jonathan Fenby, *The General: Charles de Gaulle and the France He Saved* (New York: Skyhorse Publishing, 2012), 495.
5. De Gaulle at the funeral of his youngest daughter, Anne, February 1948, quoted in Lacouture, *De Gaulle*, 142.
6. Jonathan Fenby, *The History of Modern France: From the Revolution to the War with Terror* (New York: St. Martin's Press, 2015), 461.
7. De Gaulle's radio broadcast, June 18, 1940, quoted in Lacouture, *De Gaulle*, 224–25.
8. Charles de Gaulle, *The Complete War Memoirs of Charles de Gaulle* (New York: Simon & Schuster, 1964), 92.
9. Arthur J. Marder, *Operation Menace: The Dakar Expedition and the Dudley North Affair* (New York: Oxford University Press, 1976), 143.
10. Jackson, *De Gaulle*, passim.
11. Robert and Isabelle Tombs, *That Sweet Enemy: The French and the British from the Sun King to the Present* (New York: Knopf, 2006), 569. See also Alain Larcan, *De Gaulle inventaire: la culture, l'esprit, la foi* (Paris: Bartillat, 2003), 490.
12. Winston Churchill, *Great Contemporaries* (London: Thornton Butterworth Limited, 1937), 137.
13. Richard M. Langworth, *Churchill's Wit* (London: Ebury, 2009), 69.
14. Sir Edward Louis Spears, *Fulfilment of a Mission* (Hamden, CT: Archon Books, 1977), 121.
15. François Kersaudy, *Churchill and De Gaulle* (London: Collins, 1981), 127.
16. William Craig, *Enemy at the Gates: The Battle for Stalingrad* (New York: Reader's Digest Press, 1973), xv.

17. Letter from Roosevelt to Churchill, June 17, 1943, in Warren F. Kimball, ed., *Churchill and Roosevelt: The Complete Correspondence,* vol. 2 (Princeton, NJ: Princeton University Press, 2015), 255.

18. Ibid.

19. Lewis E. Lehrman, *Churchill, Roosevelt & Company: Studies in Character and Statecraft* (Mechanicsburg, PA: Stackpole Books, 2017), 201.

20. Julian Jackson, *A Certain Idea of France: The Life of Charles de Gaulle* (London: Allen Lane, 2018), 772.

21. John Keegan, *The Second World War* (London: Pimlico, 1997), 308.

22. De Gaulle's speech after the liberation of Paris, August 25, 1944, quoted in Fenby, *The General,* 254.

23. Omar Bradley, "The German: After a Triumphant Sweep Across France," *Life,* April 23, 1951, 89.

24. Charles de Gaulle, *War Memoirs,* vol. 1, trans. Jonathan Griffin (New York: Viking Press, 1955), 9.

25. Paul Johnson, "Sinister March of the Tall Fellow," *Standpoint,* December 2015.

26. Arletty's retort during her arrest, October 20, 1944, translated as "My heart is French, but my ass is international!"

CHAPTER EIGHT: DWIGHT D. EISENHOWER

1. Bernard Montgomery of Alamein, *The Memoirs of Field Marshal Montgomery* (London: Collins, 1958), 484.

2. Field Marshal Lord Alanbrooke, *War Diaries 1939–1945,* ed. Alex Danchev and Daniel Todman (Berkeley: University of California Press, 2003), 546.

3. Rick Atkinson, "Eisenhower Rising: The Ascent of an Uncommon Man," Harmon Memorial Lecture, U.S. Air Force Academy, March 5, 2013, http://www.usafa.edu/app/uploads/Harmon55.pdf.

4. James Leasor, *War at the Top* (Cornwall, UK: House of Stratus, 2001), 298n20.

5. Rick Atkinson, *The Guns at Last Light: The War in Western Europe, 1944–1945* (New York: Henry Holt, 2013), 11–12.

6. John Colville, *The Fringes of Power: Downing Street Diaries, 1939–1955* (New York: W. W. Norton & Co., 1986), 674–75.

7. Jean Edward Smith, *Eisenhower: In War and Peace* (New York: Random House, 2012), 415.

8. Stephen E. Ambrose, *Americans at War* (New York: Berkley Books, 1997), 96.

9. Stephen E. Ambrose, *The Supreme Commander* (New York: Anchor Books, 2012), 229.

10. Atkinson, "Eisenhower Rising."

11. Atkinson, *The Guns at Last Light*, 29.

12. Winston S. Churchill, *The Second World War*, vol. 6, *Triumph and Tragedy* (Boston: Houghton Mifflin, 1953), 547.

13. Correlli Barnett, *The Lords of War: From Lincoln to Churchill* (London: The Praetorian Press, 2012), 223.

14. Stephen E. Ambrose, *Eisenhower: Soldier and President* (New York: Simon & Schuster, 1990), 126.

15. Letter from George Patton to wife, Beatrice, September 8, 1944, quoted in Martin Blumenson and Kevin M. Hymel, *Patton: Legendary Commander* (Washington, DC: Potomac Books, 2008), 68.

16. Ambrose, *Americans at War*, 136.

17. Atkinson, "Eisenhower Rising."

18. Ibid.

19. Ibid.

20. Ambrose, *Eisenhower*, 95.

21. Barnett, *The Lords of War*, 227.

22. David Irving, *The War Between the Generals* (New York: Congdon & Lattes, 1981), 94.

23. Barnett, *The Lords of War*, 229.

24. Telegraph from Churchill to Roosevelt, April 1, 1945, quoted in *Roosevelt and Churchill: Their Secret Wartime Correspondence*, ed.

Francis L. Loewenheim, Harold D. Langley, and Manfred Jonas (New York: Saturday Review Press, 1975), 699.

25. Atkinson, "Eisenhower Rising."

26. Ibid.

27. Ibid.

28. Ibid. See also "To General of the Army Dwight D. Eisenhower, May 7, 1945," in *The Papers of George Catlett Marshall*, vol. 5 (Baltimore: Johns Hopkins University Press, 2003), 168–69.

CHAPTER NINE: MARGARET THATCHER

1. Sir Lawrence Freedman, *The Official History of the Falklands Campaign*, vol. 2 (London: Routledge, 2005), 132.

2. Jorge Luis Borges, quoted in *Time*, February 14, 1983.

3. Sean Penn, "The Malvinas/Falklands: Diplomacy Interrupted," *Guardian*, February 23, 2012.

4. Max Hastings and Simon Jenkins, *The Battle for the Falklands* (London: Pan Books, 2010), 16.

5. Thatcher Archive: COI transcript, Interview for Press Association, "10th Anniversary as Prime Minister," May 3, 1989, https://www .margaretthatcher.org/document/107427.

6. Hastings and Jenkins, *The Battle for the Falklands*, 85.

7. Norman Longmate, *Island Fortress: The Defence of Great Britain, 1603–1945* (London: Random House, 2001), 267.

8. Antony Beevor, *Crete: The Battle and the Resistance* (New York: Penguin Books, 1991), 217.

9. Hastings and Jenkins, *The Battle for the Falklands*, 85.

10. Ibid., 90.

11. Ibid., 91.

12. Ibid., 102.

13. Ibid., 164.

14. Ibid., 165.

15. Ibid., 187.

16. Carol Thatcher, *Below the Parapet: The Biography of Denis Thatcher* (London: HarperCollins, 1997), 188.

17. Ibid., 320.

18. Ibid., 364.

19. Thatcher to Sir Anthony Parsons, April 18, 1982, quoted in Charles Moore, *Margaret Thatcher: The Authorized Biography*, vol. 1 (New York: Knopf, 2013), 696–97.

20. House of Commons debate, June 14, 1982, *Hansard*, vol. 25, cc700–702.

21. House of Commons debate, June 17, 1982, *Hansard*, vol. 25, cc1080–84.

22. Thatcher Archive: CCOPR 486/82, "Speech to Conservative Rally at Cheltenham," July 3, 1982, https://www.margaretthatcher.org /document/104989.

CONCLUSION: THE LEADERSHIP PARADIGM

1. Winston S. Churchill, *The World Crisis*, vol. 4, *The Aftermath, 1918–1928* (New York: Charles Scribner's Sons, 1929), 451.

2. Papers of Sir Edward Marsh, vol. 1, Churchill Archives Center, Churchill College, Cambridge.

3. Adolf Hitler, *Mein Kampf* (Archive Media Publishing, 1939), 19. See also David Dilks, *Churchill and Company: Allies and Rivals in War and Peace* (London: I. B. Tauris & Co., 2015), 267.

4. Cathal J. Nolan, *The Allure of Battle* (New York: Oxford University Press, 2017), passim.

5. Randolph Churchill, *Winston S. Churchill, Companion Volume 1, Part 2: 1896–1900* (Boston: Houghton Mifflin, 1967), 839.

6. James Gray Stuart, *Within the Fringe: An Autobiography* (London: Bodley Head, 1967), 96.

7. William I. Hitchcock, *The Age of Eisenhower: America and the World in the 1950s* (New York: Simon & Schuster, 2019), xix.

8. Roosevelt's campaign address in Boston, October 30, 1940, Master Speech File: Box 55, 1330A, https://fdrlibrary.org/.

9. Basil Liddell Hart, *Thoughts on War* (London: Faber & Faber, 1944), 222.

10. John A. Adams, *The Battle for Western Europe* (Bloomington: Indiana University Press, 2010), 200.

11. Napoleon, *Correspondance de Napoléon Ier*, ed. Henri Plon, vol. 32 (Paris: Impeimerie Impériale, 1858), 68.

12. Richard Nixon, *Leaders* (New York: Warner Books, 1982), 4.

13. Sun Tzu, *The Art of War*, trans. Lionel Giles (independently published, 2017), 10.

14. Colin White, ed., *Nelson: The New Letters* (Martlesham, UK: The Boydell Press, 2005), 160–61.

15. Ibid., 46.

16. A. J. P. Taylor, *Bismarck: The Man and the Statesman* (New York: Vintage, 1967), 115.

17. Hastings Lionel Ismay, *The Memoirs of Lord Ismay* (New York: Viking Press, 1960), 139.

18. Ibid., 140.

19. Ibid., 142.

20. Winston S. Churchill, *Great Contemporaries* (London: The Reprint Society, 1941), 304.

21. Winston Churchill, "Haig . . . the Man They Trusted," *Daily Mail*, October 3, 1935, *Daily Mail* Historical Archive.

22. Churchill's sage advice to an American exchange student, in Martin Gilbert, *Winston S. Churchill: Never Despair, 1945–1965* (London: Heinemann, 1966), 835. See also the American's recollections in James C. Humes, *Churchill: Speaker of the Century* (New York: Stein and Day, 1980), vii.

23. Terry Coleman, *The Nelson Touch: The Life and Legend of Horatio Nelson* (New York: Oxford University Press, 2002), 7.